Stories from the Turks and Caicos

Well illustrated, these fascinating stories of the older folk found inside this book are directly transcribed from video interviews.

Grammar, particularly the use of tenses and way words are said or sound are authentic and allow the reader to engage in the colloquialisms of everyday conversation from the different islands of the TCI.

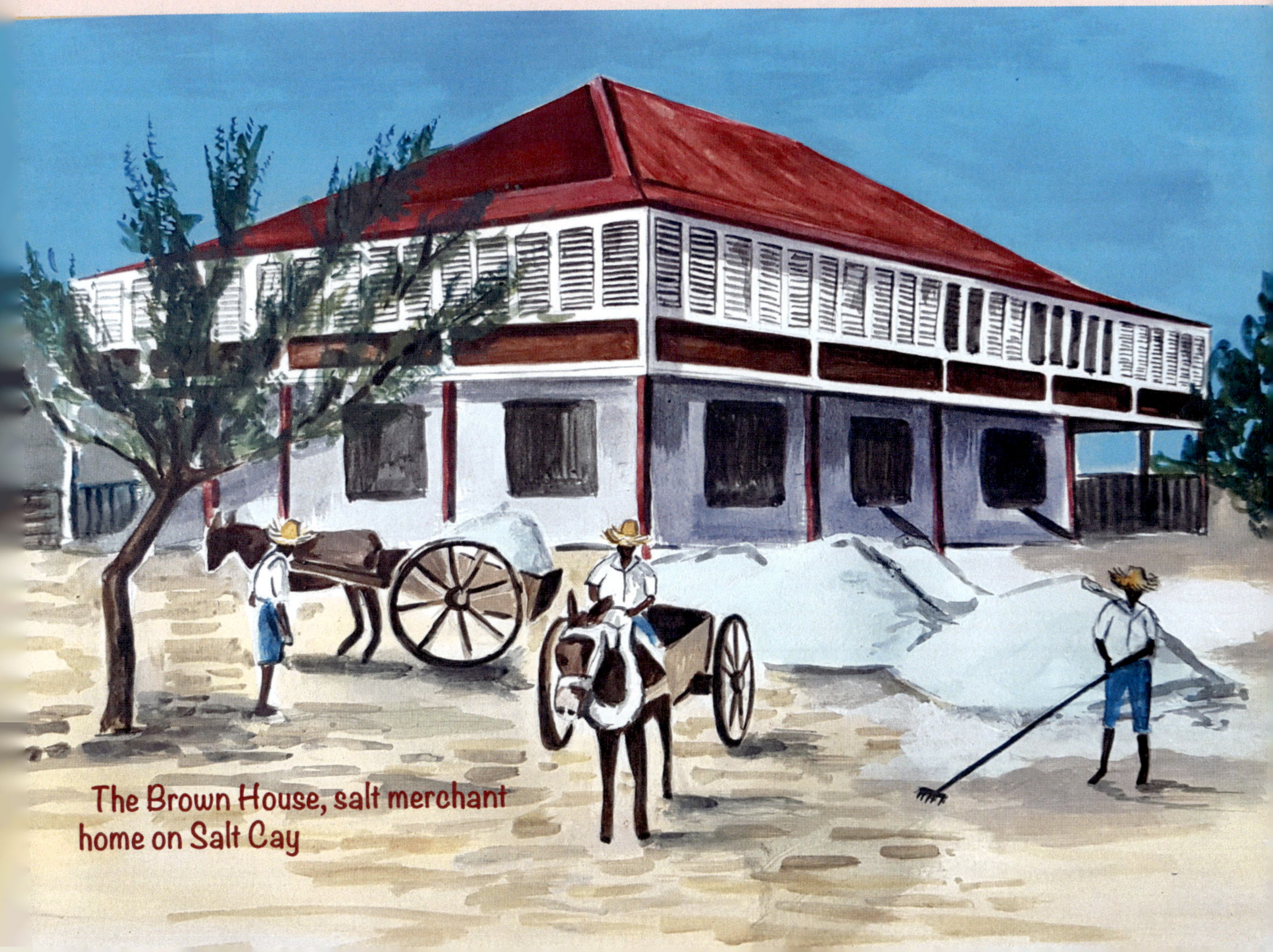

The Brown House, salt merchant home on Salt Cay

CONTENTS

I met Ms Isadora happily sitting under a tree humming to herself in 2011. She had a strong North Caicos accent and a wonderful sense of humour. It took me a long time to realize that Isadora had Alzheimer's and was quite happily living in the past.

However, this did not stop her singing, and when she began to harmonize with her husband Coletto, I was mesmerized by her melodic voice. Coletto looked on, and sat in the shade of his house shucking peas from the pods gathered in an old 'fanner' basket.

"My mother is, and my father is, still living," Isadora told me with assurance, "and they live all the way over in Belmont. It will take you all day to get there.

"My mummy name was Erica Lightbourne Henfield. She was a Lightbourne, and when I knew her she was done married twice. Her second husband, James Alexander Henfield was my father, a very strict man who rules us. We have to be humble.

"My ma, the same way. All she is, is strict, but always she gives me good advice and if we don't do as we are told, well, she will cut our tail... and I don't want my tail cut short!

"If I do not do my work right, she will beat me. I have to go over the same thing again to get it right, and let me tell you, woman, I would be sure to take my time on the next go round.

"Every day I walk to see Ma in Belmont, (a coastal village) and let me tell you the last time I saw her, she looked well to me. When I'm ready to leave her house, I say, 'Mummy I'm gone' and I walk home. Sometimes I go up in the district and visit my step aunt.

"Walking is giving you good health and makes you active. I don't like to sit up in a house, I like to use these old stick legs of mine and be active.

"Sometimes, I go to Whitby and back along the old King Road. Anytime you say you are going to Whitby, well, you might as well say that you are going for the whole day.

"My sisters I got are Gladys Taylor, Anna Henfield and Cassie and my brother's name is Jeffry Henfield. I like to visit Pa. I haven't heard anyone tell me that he's dead. He's a big fisherman. His boat was the **Sea View.**

"My grandpa is Theodore Lightbourne. Now him I haven't seen for a while! He lives down in Whitby and I must stay here in my house where I was born cos I'm the watchman for my neighbours who are gone off in the Bahamas.

"My husband Coletto, let me tell you, is a man that is used to sailing and 'fishning'(fishing) and anytime there's conch or fish about, he goes out on the boat.

I like to go fishning on the Bay and if you throw out a line, the fish are going to pick that hook up quick, and when they done swallow that hook, I've got to hit that fish to make him mine. You have to be careful because some of them fish does bite you!

"We used to eat 'filamingos'. The best time to catch them is while they are breeding. Someone has to cut off the neck and then you pick it til it's clean and then you fry it. I will give the man who caught it a portion of the meat. You have to know how to cut that filamingo up cos it's too big for the pot!

FLAMINGOS
IN THE CREEK

"Filamingo is more sweet than a chicken because they take care of themselves. They drink their water and eat their food, that's what makes them sweet. Just watch they don't pick your eyes out. So you go to the nest and get that egg so you can eat it. Just watch out for the bird cos he will tear your head off.

"In North Caicos we like to eat our crabs... rice and crabs and grits and crab. They just walk around and sometimes there are plenty of crabs in a hole. They can get real big almost so your eye can't see!

"I can tell you one thing, crabs have ten legs including their front claws. You have to be careful, because if they come on you, they will cut off half your arm.

"One day, one of those crabs did bite my finger and wouldn't let go so I had to bite out his eye.

"Let me tell you, I bite out his two eyes and left him just so. My fingers are not straight today. When that crab grabs my fingers, I am not going to holler, just drop him so, in a tin of boiling water.

"Remember you got to break open the crab and take out the fat and clean him well and good.

"When it's time for walking, they are everywhere walking around and around. When they leave from my house and go where they are going, you can walk right behind them and meet them in the bush piled up on each other.

"Let me tell you about black crows. Black crows have a nice tone of voice. If you listen you can hear him now. They have a pretty voice but black crows will eat your corn. Anything they want they are going to eat and that's why you have to cut their tail.

"You have to pull out the whole tail and just leave the rump. Well, let me tell you I carried that crow home, cleaned him up good and fried him.

"Yes man, you can eat any birds. Crows with peas and rice can be on your plate in the wink of an eye.

"Now don't give me any talking about bush medicine, I want my tea with cream and sugar. If you give me a bush tea I shall only play like I'm going to drink it."

BLACK CROW

CRABBING
IN
MIDDLE CAICOS

"I know how to plait hats from the silver-top and oh! how I love the silver-tops. Every woman who could breathe used to make hats back in the day. Once you done make your hat you go around and show everyone. 'Look what I got, let me see what you got' and so on. Each has their own design. Some favour brim, some favour fowl-head and some 'chickerbillybill.' You also plait and sew the white-top with the silver-top together. There are many ways according to what you like.

"Let's just give everyone love and a hug... that's the way to deal with people. We used to have such a nice time in the old days. People would come together in gatherings to work on our 'Programs.' They were wonderful days!

"Everybody who was in that program had the 'spirit'... they were going to have that now. In some of those programs, the people would chain in and out... a kind of a sing and dance together. You would sing and then you would reach for someone's hand and you would go in and out... chaining, that's what we does call it."

COLETTO WILLIAMS

Tough days growing up in the mid 1900s

"My father was Coletto Williams Senior, and I'se Coletto Williams Junior. My mother was Gertie Precilla Williams. Back growing up, I was subject to all different things cos times were tough. I had to go from one place to another to earn a living.

"I was living in Whitby first, and went to school in Kew. Every morning and every evening I walked to school. It took a long time to walk and sometimes it would get wet and rain and we would have to turn back and go home. Later, I left Whitby and went to live with my daddy in Grand Turk. I went to Clifford Jones school. I didn't learn much at school, my brains couldn't take it.

"School in Whitby, school in Kew and school in Grand Turk... with all the moving about, I couldn't catch hold of anything. I left school at fourteen and so when I come up to be a sizable man, well, I got into the conch business so I could make a living to help the other children. I used to go to Ambergris Cay on a small boat with two other men.

"We would have to get the conchs from the seabed, knock the conch out, shuck it out, knock the slop off and hang it up, and when it's stretched out, then you beat it, and hang it again, and eventually you take the conch to Haiti to sell.

"I remember I went on so many boats. One was called the **Mockingbird**. There was the **Sun Welcome** and the **Sea Water** and we sailed from Bottle Creek to Haiti. One time there was a terrible storm come down and the boom broke on the boat so we had to return to Port-au-Paix in Haiti. That was a scary time.

"I did not know too much about my daddy because he lived in Grand Turk. After my ma had more children this side, she sent me to him but I couldn't get along with him so I went to sea on the boats.

"My happiest days was when I changed boats and made a little money to support myself. The first boats I went out on only fed me and sent me home with nothing. I spent some hard days because I had no father to represent me.

"The first person who really helped me out was my first cousin Weston Williams, but he's dead now. He was the first person to take me away from the boats where I was not paid. He would carry me on trips to Haiti, gave me clothes and money and taught me what man and life is about.

"When I finished with the conching, I went to work on Inagua Island to do contract work with the Ericsson Company.*

"Sometimes I would take trips to Salt Cay in the sail boats. We would carry blades to the Morgans. They were big salt proprietors on Salt Cay and used the blades to feed the mules which would carry the salt from the ponds to land.

*Many Turks Islands went to Inagua seeking employment. At one time the Ericsson Brothers had bought the abandoned salt ponds from the British government to redevelop the salt trade.

Tribute to the artist:
Winslow Homer
1836-1910

"We would make small bundles of blades and Morgan would pay us one shilling a hundred. Sometimes it would take three days to reach Salt Cay. You would have to sail round the land and go up to South Caicos, and from there you go on the ocean and go Salt Cay.

"Even though the blades were all dried up from the heat of the boat, the merchant took it from us. We used to go into Deans Dock, moor our boats and throw the grass on the land.

"Morgan had a servant to receive everything and we would go in his office to get paid. His office was right there in a two storey house by the dock which I believe was called Mt Pleasant.

"He was a light skinned man and treated us well. He would give us a bag of corn from the animal house to carry back to North Caicos with us. He was a kind man and he wasn't proud... he treat us good.

"I would not like to work in the salt ponds. I could see how the men got on. They were standing up in that hot brine all day and sometimes with no shoes.

"Believe me, I was not jealous of that. They used to work from seven o'clock to nine in the evening. The windmills used to turn the water on and off the ponds. Everything depended on good timing and the weather.

"I never met the Harriotts, but the old man got drowned sailing over to the North point of Salt Cay. He was coming from Grand Turk with money to pay off his workers, but the boat got swamped and he drowned right there.

Salt Cay has a dangerous reef and when sea capping on that reef, you may not make it. Harriott was a good boatsman but when sea rough, sea rough and don't mind how good you be!"

Loading salt into the mule carts on Salt Cay

It Is Well with My Soul

When peace like a river attendeth my way,
When sorrows like sea billows roll;
Whatever my lot, Thou hast taught me to say,
It is well, it is well with my soul.

It is well with my soul,
It is well, it is well with my soul.

Though Satan should buffet, though trials
should come, let this blest assurance control,
That Christ hath regarded my helpless estate,
And hath shed His own blood for my soul.

My sin—oh, the bliss of this glorious thought!
My sin, not in part but the whole,
Is nailed to the cross, and I bear it no more,
Praise the Lord, praise the Lord, O my soul!

For me, be it Christ, be it Christ hence to live.
If Jordan above me shall roll,
No pang shall be mine, for in death as in life
Thou wilt whisper Thy peace to my soul.

But, Lord, 'tis for Thee, for Thy coming we wait,
The sky, not the grave, is our goal;
Oh, trump of the angel! Oh, voice of the Lord!
Blessed hope, blessed rest of my soul!

It is well with my soul, and Lord, haste
the day when the faith shall be sight,
The clouds be rolled back as a scroll;
The trump shall resound, and the Lord
shall descend,
Even so, it is well with my soul.

The Complex Life Cycle of the Great Blue Land Crab

These blue land crabs are found throughout the Caribbean Sea, Brazil, Columbia, Bahamas and along the Mexican and Florida coastlines.

They are semi-terrestrial crabs and are adapted for life along low lying coastlines and flourish well in the Turks and Caicos Islands especially in coastal areas where the natural habitat is undisturbed by development.

Like all crabs, the great blue land crab is a type of crustacean sharing similar characteristics with prawns, shrimp, crayfish and lobster.

One of the shared features of these crustaceans is the hard exoskeleton (shell), which is important for protecting the animal from predators and water loss.

This protective shell is known as a carapace and on the great blue land crab can grow to a width of around six inches. Protruding out on stalks are the bulbous socket-less eyes.

Another shared characteristic with other male crabs is the growth of one extra large claw called a dimorphic claw which is particularly handy for excavating burrows, self protection, attracting females and gathering food.

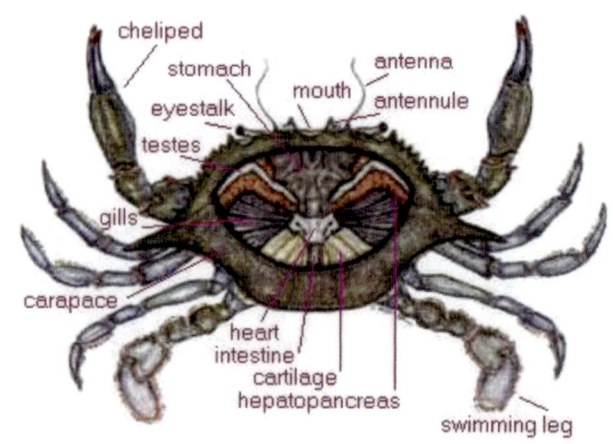

In the quiet settlements on North Caicos and particularly Middle Caicos, a high number of Great Blue Crabs are found near the ponds, mangroves, muddy flats and sandy beaches where they can dig deep burrows in which to live and hide.

The burrows not only help protect the crabs from the elements and predators, but also lead to pools of water, a life-giving element essential for the welfare of the crab!

The reproductive cycle is linked to the weather. At the end of May and with the fall of heavy spring rains these crabs emerge from their burrows for their migration phase. This first involves scavenging for fruit, flowers, decaying plants and sometimes insects, beetles and other small soft-shelled crabs.

They are not fussy eaters and eat like humans, using their claws to push food into their mouths. They like to feed at night and possess a well developed sense of taste and smell. Crabs find food by light and sound detectors and by feeling vibrations through chemo receptors located on the their antennae.

During the migration period, blue crabs can be very disruptive to the local homesteads. As Isadora Henfield Williams once told me, "you have to chase them out the house and yard or they will pick you with their claws."

In actual fact, land crabs are shy and it takes around four years for the males to reach sexual maturity. By mid summer the mature males are ready for mating and transfer sperm into the female by an internal fertilization process.

The adult female then lays her eggs and carries them en masse beneath her body. After a couple of weeks the female makes her way to the ocean to release the eggs into the shallow waters where thousands of eggs are spawned.

The larvae then float out to sea and within a month the larvae develop into small crabs, at which point the currents and tides carry them back to shore.

However, very few larvae survive the watchful eye of the fish and bird predators that love to feast on nutritious baby crabs.

REPAIRING THE FISHING NETS

Like her grandparents and parents before her, Ms Mary Outten has lived in the settlement of Lorimers all her life.

Even to this day, Ms Mary carries on the long family tradition of farming and caring for the Mt Herman Baptist Church.

Born on the 8th February 1928, Ms Mary was the youngest of five children. Her mother was named Mary Augusta Tucker Hall and was a strict, stout woman who was the school superintendent and on Sunday mornings one of her duties was to raise the hymns.

"She used to teach the congregation," Mary said, "and tell us children about the bible, chapters and verse.

"She learnt us plenty of things. I remember, her favorite song was 'Praise the Saviour.'

MARY ALICE HALL OUTTEN

From the settlement of Lorimers in Middle Caicos

Back in the day Middle Caicos was known as Grand Caicos as it was the largest island in the Turks and Caicos.

There were three main settlements, one of which was Lorimers. The village was named after a British military doctor and plantation owner by the name of John Lorimer.

Upon his death, John's Will stated that his slaves were to be freed and to mark this occasion, they named the village after him.

PRAISE THE SAVIOUR 1806

Praise the Savior, ye who know Him!
Who can tell how much we owe Him?
Gladly let us render to Him
All we are and have.

Jesus is the name that charms us;
He for conflicts fits and arms us;
Nothing moves and nothing harms us
When we trust in Him.

Trust in Him, ye saints, forever;
He is faithful, changing never;
Neither force nor guile can sever
Those He loves from Him

Then we shall be where we would be;
Then we shall be what we should be;
Things which are not now, nor could be,
Then shall be our own.

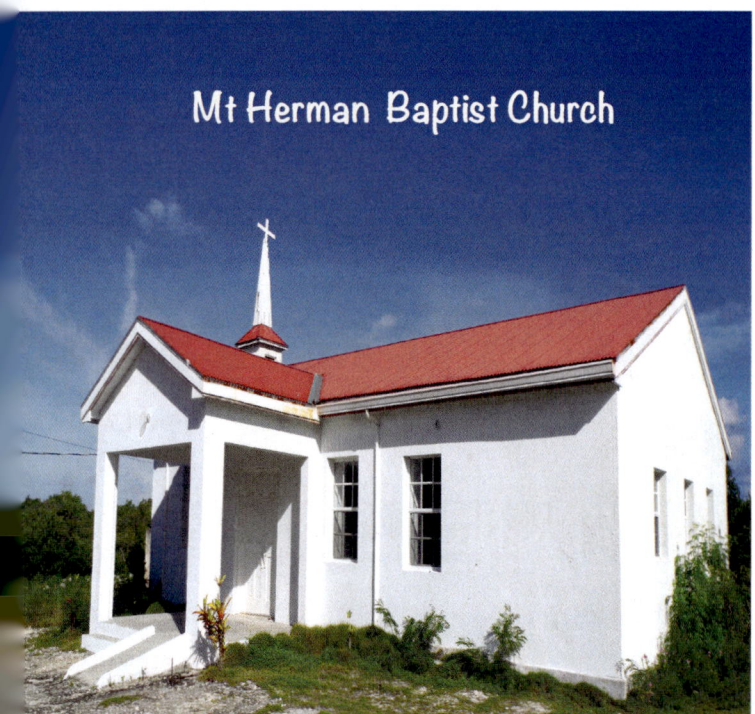

Mt Herman Baptist Church

"My grandfather," said Ms Mary, "was Stephan Hall who was my father's daddy. He worked field but was also the deacon of the Church until he could no longer and die. He would keep service and take good care of the congregation.

"I never knew my grandma because she died before I was born. She worked field and had many children but they all died out one by one.

"That left my daddy. His name was Marcelino Hall. He was a farmer and had a little shop in the yard. We called them 'boutie' because they were small. Atha wife of Sammy Missick had one.

"My father was also the organist in Mt Herman. A lady from here by the name of Clarinda Parker used to teach music and my father went to her to learn the notes.

"He became very popular and he was able to play in the church every Sunday while the congregation sang all the old Sankey songs.

"My oldest brother Stephan also played, and he tried to learn me, but my fingers were so short I couldn't reach the keys.

"I could play a couple of tunes, but not to say play in the Church. Stephan finally left for the Bahamas like many of the young men.

"When I was a little girl, I used to go to school. My teacher was Peter Hall and every morning we had to do devotions, go to the local well to collect water for bathing and start the cooking. Then we rushed to get ready to walk to school before we were late.

"Peter's brother Daniel Hall kept school in Kew. He's the one that got 'drown-ded' (drowned) in the 65 hurricane.

"When they were going up South Caicos, the hurricane came down. There had not been a hurricane for sixteen years and the men were not expecting it.

"Many people got drowned, four men from Lorimers and many from Blue Hills. They are better prepared these days but hurricanes are not a pretty sight.

"I remember the strong men would walk around in the community to see how families were surviving. They struggled through the heavy rain and wind. They could tell you whose house fall and whose house stand. Those who died, died at sea.

"When the people die on land we have a public cemetery. If people died early in the day, we try to bury them same day. If they die late in the day, we wait for the morrow.

"We had no morgue to put them in. In those days some would dig the holes and others would make the cords to lower the coffin.

"And then we would call Church to the cemetery and sing songs from the Sankey hymn book. Back then it was a lively settlement, everyone farming and going to Church.

"When I was just twenty, I married a local man by the name of Telford Garnett Outten. We had fifteen children, but only nine survived. Like my brother, Telford left to the Bahamas to find work leaving me to raise the children.

"This was very usual for men and women to leave the home. At one time we had a lot of people in Lorimers. They went to Nassau and Miami, and when Blue Hills and Providenciales got a new project building roads, many folk went there to get some livelihood.

"Back in those days everyone was doing farming. We would grow corn and peas, potatoes, pumpkins, tomatoes... there were many vegetables and fruit. At that time you raised the food, but you could get very little money for it.

"The food was carried to the other Turks islands but it was sold for little or nothing. There was so little work round here.

"At Christmas you were given a little road work or weeding so you'se could get a little something but that was no money at all. They were not easy times.

"I would work the shop, tend field, make hats and baskets to sell in Grand Turk. I would sew clothes on my mother's old Singer machine. I would make all my children's clothes. The cloth would come from Grand Turk and Haiti.

"The fishermen took their dried conch to Haiti to sell but when they came home the boats were full of odds and ends like dyed cottons, yarns, barrels of salt-beef, rice, flour and lard which we needed for cooking.

"When Daphne Hall and Simon Hall were living, Simon was the chief deacon of Mt Herman. When he died Richard Robinson took over, but he sickened and left to Nassau. Alton Higgs became the new chief and he still keeps Church, but my son Garnett is now the chief deacon.

"As a child, I played with many friends and when we were allowed by my mother, we went swimming over by the creek near Lorimers Landing. We could watch the men fishing with their line and hook... women too sometimes.

"We didn't have toys what like they have today but we had fun playing tag, dancing round the maypole and making rag doll baby girls at Christmas.

"We were a lucky family though because my pa had the little shop in the yard. For many years I run that shop and kept it supplied with all the necessary things.

Sponge Fleet Nassau

"There's not many homes in Lorimers now, but still I stay here. I am eighty two years old, and on welfare and that's why I am out in the road weeding. The pay is so small but I get a couple of dollars. I work for three days a week and that helps out with my National.

"When I was a child, the first preacher I remember was Billy Tucker. He was a fair man that used to preach well.

"When you see the new year come, everyone wanted him to preach. After him came Simon Hall and then Samuel Missick, Alton Higgs and then my son. All my children preach. I had six boys.

"When you born them, you have to teach them to serve the Lord and grow up in the Church so that they may also teach their children.

"The problem today is that the children are not disciplined. They are different from our days. They have gone far away from the teaching.

"They pass you in the road and not say good morning or good day and so on. Yes, today the children will look up in your eye, pass you by, and not say one word. The parents are letting the children have too much of their own way.

"The bible says, 'train up the child when he is young and when they get older they will not depart from the Church. When you train them small, they will grow up in the right way.'

"I had two brothers and two sisters but both sisters died young. My sister Cassandra died when she went to the neighbour's house to roast corn.

"You know when you roast corn some-times, the fire gets on the nerve of the corn and flames up. My sister paid no attention and the flame lit her dress.

"She tried to run home but the breeze blew up and fanned the fire. She told her mother that she was calling her but none could hear her, and when they looked out the window she was ablaze.

"My sister lived ten days but the burns got to her and she didn't survive. There were no doctors back then and I wonder how people survived... only by the grace of God.

"I had another sister called Sophia who died young when she was cutting teeth. Some children cut teeth really bad which makes them weak and they die. The store sold teething powder but this did not work. When women were pregnant they had the help of midwives who used root medicine.

"In my time there used to be a lady by the name of Sue Jennings who knew all the root remedies. There was another lady by the name of Almara Outten who was sent to Jamaica to train as a midwife. She stayed here in Middle Caicos until she was old, and then the children took her to Grand Turk.

"Bush medicine... there is one called wowine and they say when you drink that bush it's good for the pressure. It grows commonly about. I put some aside while I was pulling weed this morning.

"There was a bush we used called catnip and when the woman delivered her baby she was always given catnip to drink.

"They have another medicine called a winder that they would put in a pitcher which they said was 'coolin.' People would constantly drink that. Sometimes your urine get so red that you would drink the winder until your urine get clear.

"Now when you have pain in your stomach then you use snake stick. This bush medicine is good for you. You get the stick of the root and strip it. Then cut it up in a cup of water and 'steep' it. Thats what we call it, and when you think it bitter enough, you drink it. With a little Lord inside it, you will feel better.

"Five finger bush is also here about. This is good for making tea. When you let it dry and steep it in water, it taste something like green tea. We use this for backaches.

"Cerasse is just like the bay tansy which are winders that grows on the bay. It's good for fever and used for many other things. I still drink bush tea from time to time and I enjoy sitting down with a nice cup of cerasse tea.

"When I was young I used to go on the sailing boats to Grand Turk and sometimes it would take two days. The men who had boats were from the next settlement, called Bambarra. They built the sloops to go to Grand Turk. Here in Lorimers we only had little dinghy boats to go to South Caicos.

"There were a lot of shops in South, owned by the Ewings, Andrew Towers, Annie Stubbs and many more. They used to sell dry goods and grocery. From Grand Turk we would buy materials like gingham and chambord.

"This fabric we used to make tough clothes for the hard work, like for when I go weeding on the roads. We always wore hats, and on Sunday we wore shop hats.

"In the old days, the dresses we wore to the knees or just below the knees. We used to wear what we called undercoats. Many of us used to sew... I myself made my own clothes. It was my mother taught me how to sew and cook and make baskets and hats.

"On a Saturday we used to make souse and a bread we called loaf-bread. Souse is a kind of broth with scraps of chicken or pig inside, pickled like.

Credit to Artist, Elmer Joseph Read

"After church on Sunday, we go home and prepare Irish potato and sometimes if it's season we make hash lobster. If you have a cabbage then we make cabbage slaw.

"On Monday you would make soup and things. I never did like dumplings in my soup. And then again, all the week you could've got fish plentiful to eat.

"I remember though during the wartime, it was difficult to find many dry goods that came from away. You could not get lard for cooking.

"Nowadays, they have cooking oil to cook with, but back then we made do with lard to make the shortening and fry the fish.

"So what we people did was to go on the Bay, and pick up something called 'tanger,' which was something like grease. Back then, people found barrels of this fat. It was drift that washed ashore. We put this grease into small containers and used this when it was needed for frying.

Walking the Bay for drift

"Most times though, the tanger would turn hard. I have never known where the drift came from but maybe from ships wrecked at sea.

"Every day we walked to the school here in Lorimers where Peter Hall was the head teacher. Peter had a daughter called Sula married to Julius Baker in Grand Turk.

"We had to learn poetry and recite it out loud. I remember him telling me this story about a woman having a crippled son.

"She would set him to a window every day and he had to stay there until he was moved.

"However", continued Mary Outten, "one day the crippled child asked his mother, *Oh mother, why has God made me so? What use am I, what work is mine? And then his tears would flow.*

"The mother you see was feeling the sorrow of her son and decided to give him these comforting words. She told him: *Nay nay my child be patient still, be sure these words are true, God has a plan for every man and he has one for you.*

"Our school recitation", said Mary, "because the child was crippled he could not move around like other children. That's why he asked his mother for an explanation. The young boy couldn't run, he couldn't play and he couldn't earn any money to help his family.

"The mother wanted to reassure him that he was not alone in the world and forgotten. The poem explains that everyone on earth is important to God and that a plan exists for all.

"I am sure our teacher Peter Hall made us learn this dissertation in school to teach us that you should never be discouraged in life because **God has a plan for every man.**"

18

Mary Outten
in her
periwinkle
garden

Historically, the periwinkle plant has been used as a bush medicine throughout the West Indies and is still used to treat a number of health issues.

However, the plant is sometimes called the flower of death because it contains naturally-occurring toxic alkaloids which can be poisonous when ingested.

Even so, Mary Outten told me that 'grannies' often brewed a concoction of periwinkle flowers to drink as a cough medicine. "Sometimes," she said, "you can boil the leaves and place over a wound and it slows down the bleeding. It can stop the sting from insect bites. We have plenty of biting mosquitoes around here and periwinkle is a good remedy to prevent itch and inflammation.

"I have plenty of periwinkles in my garden."

THE HARMLESS TURKS & CAICOS RAINBOW BOA

Chilabothrus chryogastor

Contrary to local, popular belief, the Turks and Caicos Rainbow Boa, scientifically called ***Chilabothrus chrysogaster,*** is a harmless and non-venomous snake that lives mainly in the Caicos Islands and on Inagua, Crooked Island and Acklins in the Bahamas. Previously they were spotted on Grand Turk and Providenciales but as both towns developed for the tourist industry, the boas disappeared.

They are nicknamed 'Rainbow Boa' because of the prismatic shimmer on their scales seen clearly in the sunlight. For the most part though, island boas are nocturnal, preferring to hunt for their food at night foraging for small critters like small birds, geckos and lizards.

Like all snakes, the boas are carnivores, and swallow their catch whole by flexing their jaw, which allows them to swallow critters like mice and rats that have a habit of moving into settlement areas.

In days gone by these snakes scared villagers, and this often resulted in the snake's untimely demise by a sharp whack to the head.

Before the heavy development began in the 1970s, the ecosystems of the Turks and Caicos were ideal habitats for these slender boas which can grow to over five feet long with a colour of mainly grey, spotted with brown irregular blotches. The juveniles by contrast have an orangey, reddish skin.

In the day time, boas rest and hide from predators under large limestone rocks or stumps of old trees and logs, preferring the biomes of scrub vegetation and dry forest habitats.

Today the biggest threat to the survival of the rainbow boa is habitat loss through coastal development, road construction and increased population.

In fact, the continued unspoilt habitat on Middle, North and Ambergris Cay is one reason why these snakes are still found.

The presence of boulders that scatter the islands also provides an advantage point for hunting unsuspecting prey and shading the boas from the hot day sun.

Other threats remain the predatory wild dogs and cats and the risk of attack by homeowners who do not realize that these boas are completely harmless.

Rainbow Boa , Turks and Caicos

21

Isadora Henfield Williams had this to say about the boa...

"You only see snakes when they are mating, when they are together like.

"I'm not scared of snakes but if they are right behind me I am not going to run. I shall hold my ground and lick them snakes down with my stick.

"I always keep a big stick handy. If I had my dog with me I can tell you that I wouldn't have to fight that snake so hard.

"I still take the stick with me because I wouldn't want the snake to kill my dog."

2010 Mathew Niemillar (photo credit)

"My mother's name was Rosina Francis and my father was Zachus Gibson, but I did not know him because he died before I born. He came from Eluthera and was a conch diver. He came this way and settled in Middle Caicos where my ma met him.

"She never married him, but she had a lot of children, and she worked very hard to raise them with the Strength of God. Likewise, she taught us to work hard for our children. We burn coal, we cut sisal, we worked farm, and we raised produce with the help of God.

"Every day we helped my ma. We were only little children but we had enough sense to help ma on the farm. We used to grow corn, peas, cassava and potato.

"My mummy was a young, short woman and very helpful. She was a kind woman. She would say 'Effie, be kind to people. If you have a piece of bread, you must share it. If you go to a person's home and they cleaning, help them.

Ms EFFIE HALL

From the settlement of Kew in North Caicos

Water Carriers

"'They will say "no" but help them anyway. They may say "let me pay you" but you must say no. You will get more blessings from God that will come back threefold.'

"Even today, if I have only one piece of corn, I will break it and share it. That's what my mummy teach us. She taught us how to share and how to pray.

"Everyone of her children had to say 'Our Father's Prayer' every morning when we wake up. I am a Christian lady through my mother's teaching. Today I can pray over the offering and I always thank God for providing for me.

"I did not have much learning when I was a little girl but my brother did go to school. My mother wanted me to fix like other children, but we were too poor and I ended up on the farm growing sweet peppers and so on.

"I worked there with Annie Gardener who lives close by, and many other labourers. There was Ms Cornelia but she die, and mummy Dean.

"There was also many from Bottle Creek. We used pick axe, we used fork, we used little hand shovels to dig holes and plant produce.

"We worked really hard for very little money, and barely enough to raise the children, but with the help and grace of the Almighty God we made it.

"I had ten children to raise besides two that were born but did not live. When my last daughter Evette was born, I was living in a place called Hall Town.

"In the old days we used to cut the sisal, soak it, beat it, clean it, and go to South Caicos where there used to be a company that would buy the sisal.

The sisal was then sent to Jamaica and different places. We used to make the mats, slippers and hats out of sisal but we always called sisal by the name 'Manilla'.

3c SISAL INDUSTRY

TURKS & CAICOS
ISLANDS

"I used to make rope. We used to have what we call a 'Jack'... one over there, and another a distance away. You get a couple of labourers who have to stretch the sisal by keep turning the jack.

"They just keep turning... then you twist the sisal into rope. Many old time ships used long lengths of rope for the sails.

"First, the sisal has to be washed in the sea. Now you had to make a big crawl and split the manilla, tie them up in bundles and put the bundles in the crawl to let them soak.

"The crawl is in the water. It's like a cage with the manilla soaking inside. You have to tie the bundles so they don't wash away on the tide. You also put large sticks on top of the bundles to hold the manilla in place.

"Then we go in the crawl and pat all the shuck off the manilla to clean it like. You take a piece of board and keep tapping the manilla til it looks white, and when it's clean you dry it.

"When it's in the bundles you would say 'this is for five dollars or this is for ten dollars.'

"Sometimes we would send our bundles to South Caicos with our names written on it. We worked through an agent.

"Ms Celia Robinson down the road, well, her husband was an agent for the company in South Caicos. We used to sell the sisal to him.

"We also sold to Mr Isa Wyns and his wife. They would buy big bundles and put a tag on and send them onwards to South Caicos on the boats. The agent there was Mr Bob Francis.

"When I was younger, I was married to a man they called Samuel Hall. He was first married to a lady in the Bahamas, but after they couldn't see eye to eye he came back home and married me.

"Back then a lot of men went to the Bahamas to find work and send money home to support the family. After we married, I had ten children. My eldest and youngest die, but I have three daughters in Miami and three daughters in Provo.

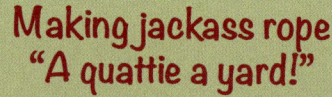

Making jackass rope
"A quattie a yard!"

"Now I can remember one song that my mummy learn me:- *'When I was young my mother told me, say child don't worry, just put your hand in Jesus hand and he will lead you to the end.'*

"I always remember these words from my mother. She used to always say that it does not matter how dark the way may seem, just go to your bedside, kneel and pray.

"God will open the windows and doors and help you find the light.

"My mother taught me how to plait hats. You take the white top from the palm and strip it. These strips are sewed together to make the hat. It takes two days and a night to make a hat if you can plait really quick.

25

"The top tree has brown berries. When the berries are full and ripe, we pick them and put them in a bottle and make wine. You add water to the bottle and about four grains of corn.

"You 'stop' the bottle and put it in the sun and wait for it to draw. You know when it's ready because it's dark in colour. The next step is you strain it and sweeten it, and then you drink it and let me tell you that's nice!

Carrying sisal to the Bay

"Let me show you what I knit. It takes me two nights and longer for the fringe. We grew up sewing, making little dresses and shirts for the children. I made little shorts with apron fronts for the boys.

"From the top tree, you can also plait baskets. First you cut the blades and then you need to dry them out. This takes about four or five days. I have some in the house that I can show you.

"Once the palm is dry, then you can strip them down into lengths so that you can start. There are all kinds of different ways to plait. The one I am showing you here is what we call a 'Centipeder Belly.'

"Once we have done the plaiting, we varnish, just the same as you use for chairs. In the old days many of us knew how to make hats and baskets but nowadays there is few of us left.

"See the basket I show you... well, Ms Duncan did that. She can make any kind of basket you want and one large enough for all your clothes to take a trip to Provo.

"She made the rope handle out of sisal, and she made a pretty lining out of cotton.

Effie Hall demonstrating the 'Centipeder Belly' Stitch

"I sent my children to Church with clothes that I made with my hands. My mother also taught me about bush medicine. There are many, and one of them we use a lot, right up until today is snake-stick.

"If you have a bad pain in your stomach, break some off that snake stick, hot some water in a cup and add the sticks. When that has steeped woman, then you drink that down. That pain in the stomach with the Lord in it, is going to ease your worries.

"Now if you go by the seaside you can find what we call the crab-bush. You keep on chewing this and you swallow the juice. This is good for griping and will make you feel more better.

"There are plenty of little bushes that you can make tea from, and one I like is dill seed with basely bush, which is good for indigestion and makes you feel better."

"Because my mother wasn't married she had a hard life but we all helped her in many ways. She would say, 'Child, keep your surroundings clean because you never know when someone pop up to your place.'

"I bought my children up in the House of the Lord. I can only tell you to keep to the straight and narrow. The truth is the truth and that's what people should live by.

"Some mothers have it so that the children rule them, but when my kids were under my wine and fig tree, I was the one who ruled.

"I don't joke with children. When my grand children come to visit, they know what 'grammy' stand for:-

Truth Respect and Love."

ALL ALONE

On Mount Olive's sacred brow
Jesus spent the night in pray'r,
He's the pattern for us all, all alone,
If we'll only steal away
In some portion of the day,
We will find it always pays to be alone.

Refrain:
There are times I'd like to be
All alone with Christ my Lord,
I can tell Him of my troubles all alone.

There are times I'd like to be
With the sanctified and blest,
There are times I like to be all alone,
God can always grace impart,
To my weary, saddened heart,
There are times I'd like to be just all alone.

When a heart is broken up
With the tearful, lonesome cup,
Then's the time to go to Christ all alone,
In our blessed Lord divine,
There is peace and joy sublime,
When we take our sorrows all to Him alone.

Above is the favorite hymn of Effie Hall written by a Methodist minister from Georgia by the name of George Thomas Byrd in the year 1871.

Beautiful
hand- made hats
from the Islands

30

AMERICAN WAR OF INDEPENDENCE

Who were the Loyalists or King's Men?

King George III.
Portrait by Allan Ramsay, 1762

The American War of Independence, also known as the American Revolution, began in April 1775 and was fueled by the growing discontent in England's thirteen North American colonies.

Their anger was directed against the monarchy and the British parliament, which was enacting unfavourable laws by imposing heavy taxes and unpopular measures of control on the colonies.

In fact, this tension had been steadily mounting since before the outbreak of war. King George III, also known as mad King George, was the king of England and had succeeded his grandfather George II.

The latter had regrettably left the treasury in significant debt from financing a series of wars with France and Spain and spending considerable sums of money on expanding the British territories globally.

Needless to say, the King's government faced the challenge of reducing the national debt.

His Prime Minister, George Grenville, who was also First Lord of the Treasury, declared that substantial funds could be raised from taxing the colonies, who had hitherto enjoyed a laissez-faire style of governing themselves.

Resentment came to a head with the Stamp Act, which was passed by the British parliament on March 22, 1765. The new tax was imposed on American colonists and required them to pay tax on all printed paper including ship's papers, legal documents, licenses, newspapers and even leisure items like playing cards.

Denouncing the Stamp Act

Two years later Charles Townshend, the Chancellor of the Exchequer, exacerbated the unrest by introducing the Townshend Acts which imposed custom duties on popular imported goods like glass, paints, paper and tea.

The colonists were most upset and pushed for a revolution especially because they had no representation in the British parliament. Their slogan was 'no taxation without representation.'

It soon became clear that taxing tea was a huge mistake as tea was considered a necessary household commodity.

The result culminated in the famous Boston Tea Party protest in which Samuel Adams and the Sons of Liberty boarded three ships in the Boston harbour and threw 342 chests of tea overboard.

Soon cries of 'liberty' could be heard on the streets and a division of loyalties began to split the colonies in two.

The families that supported the cry for independence were called patriots, sons of liberty, whigs and colonists. They argued that a break away from British rule would benefit the colonies.

In the opposing camp, the men and women who wanted to remain British citizens and stay loyal to the King were called loyalists, tories or the king's men.

It stands to reason that the many merchants who had business interests with England feared that separation would destroy trade.

When the war ended in 1783 and the patriots had declared victory, Great Britain signed the Treaty of Paris on September 3rd declaring the 'United States of America.'

By this time, many of the loyalists had fled the colonies and were settling in Florida to escape hostility and victimization.

However, soon after the peace treaty was signed Florida was returned to the Spanish, and once again the loyalists felt obliged to move further afield.

This dramatic political upheaval changed the course of history and its cause and effect reached the shores of the Bahamas and the Caicos Islands.

Under the 5th article of the Treaty, the loyalists were given eighteen months to dispose of their land, collect any debts, gather together their few possessions and move to other regions in the British Empire.

Many families made their way to Canada in order to build a new and better life. Some of the more successful business men took the arduous journey to England in order to re-establish ties, business concerns and trading.

However, the Southern loyalists from Georgia, South Carolina and nearby states decided to go further South to the West Indies, the Bahamas, Jamaica, Abaco and the Caicos Islands where they could cultivate the land, and grow cash crops.

These loyalists already had experience as farmers and plantation owners and felt they could succeed. The Caicos Islands, in truth, had been deserted since the days when the Taino settlements had been completely wiped out by the Spanish invaders.

Later, the nooks and crannies of the Caicos islands were a favourite hiding place for pirates and privateers patrolling the area for ships and loot.

Many loyalists were in fact induced to the islands by reports from a certain Lieutenant Wilson who had been commissioned to scout the uncultivated land ahead of the loyalists' arrival.

In his report, Wilson declared the land agreeable for growing a number of fruits, tobacco and cotton.

In many cases, grants of land known as 'free of quit' were offered to the loyalists and with this added incentive they set about clearing, seeding and sprouting the land with guinea corn, yams, potatoes and other vegetables.

The more experienced cotton growers from the southern colonies grew cotton, for they knew this to be a profitable crop and in great demand along the trade routes to England.

This new influx of settlers with their enslaved labourers would, in many ways, shape the next chapter in the future development of the Caicos Islands.

Surrender at York Town

LIFE ON THE CAICOS PLANTATIONS

Many of the enslaved who arrived on the Caicos Islands would have made yet another traumatic move leaving behind family members and established kinship patterns in America. The confusion of departure on a ship voyage into the unknown, and arriving on an island void of people, houses and crops would have been terrifying and disheartening.

The loyalists came. Every tool, utensil, food item and necessities needed for survival on a remote island would have arrived on board the ships, along with the enslaved, animals, and an assortment of barrels, drums and furniture.

Many of the loyalists were military men used to strict discipline and hardship. Others were already experienced planters from Georgia.

Their slaves ploughed and toiled the soil from sun up to sun down, preparing the land, destroying weed and bush and finally in February planting the cotton. In later months, the cotton was thinned, handpicked and 'ginned' to take out the seeds from the soft wool.

During this time, the enslaved built the stone-walled plantation houses along the coast, and the Kings Highway was forged in North Caicos providing a main road and pathways to the merchants' homes, harbour, loading bays and ships.

The enslaved assembled their own quarters away from the main house. Often the walls were made of rocks and mortar mixed from lime and bay sand and the roof made from 'thatch' from the local palm leaves.

On the plantations they would grow guinea corn, pigeon peas, okra, yams, sweet potato and other vegetables. Many of the plants were originally known on the African shores.

'Grits' was the staple diet made from dried and coarsely ground guinea corn. Without the hull, the grits were called 'homini,' although the words were often interchangeable.

The men would supplement the homini with the odd fish, conch and turtle, which were plentiful at the time.

The enslaved brought with them their own knowledge of bush medicine and grew medicinal plants near their homes like catnip, cerasee and fever grass.

Each leaf, bud, bark and flower made a 'cooling' or hot tea and provided a topical remedy for many ailments caused by the harsh conditions.

Gradually, over time, the community grew and kinship patterns formed.

Days off were rare, and were cause for resting and singing. They sang songs derived from the gospel and from rhythmic songs shared while working in the fields. They told old stories passed on from their ancestors and no doubt recounted the incidents of the day.

Everyone was multi-tasking, working hard in the plantations weaving baskets, fetching water, nursing the young and sick, raising livestock and tending the mules, pigs and other livestock.

Skilled tradesmen were always needed, like carpenters, blacksmiths and cart-wrights who would repair the wheels and wagons that were often broken.

Broken because the carts were often laden down with cotton bales ready for transportation and transfer to the ships.

A day's work was always long and arduous with harsh punishments from brutal overseers. Always there were the endless dreams of running away to freedom and a better life.

Lemon Grass known as Fever Grass

WADE STUBBS

A loyalist, cotton planter in North Caicos

One such loyalist planter was a man by the name of Wade Stubbs who fled Florida in 1789 and set about growing a cotton plantation on North Caicos called 'Wades Green.'

On his arrival to the Caicos, his slaves were required to build the plantation house, slave quarters and out-buildings from local limestone found in abundance across the hitherto virgin land.

Even though life was relatively better then other plantations, many workers attempted to escape, and often Wade Stubbs posted in the Bahama Gazette offering rewards for the return of his slaves.

"Escaped, by the names of Manual, a tall slim man of about 5' 10'', African born with many of his country marks on his face, speaks French fluently but little English. Also escaped a small negro named Dublin from the same country as Manual. They carried with them an open sail boat, drawing about two feet of water, Bermuda built and all plank and timbers made of cedar. She sailed only with a 'shoulder of mutton' sail.

"A reward of fifty dollars is offered for each negro found. Any information about the said runaways will be thankfully acknowledged by Wade Stubbs. Grand Caicos. February 28 1794."

During his lifetime, Wade Stubbs was well known in Nassau. He was considered a prominent planter in the region.

When he died in 1822, it is recorded that he owned 384 slaves and over eight thousand acres of land.

Without a doubt, living on the Caicos islands was challenging on every front. Often droughts and high winds were detrimental to the crops and perhaps the most damaging news for the planters was the depletion of the cotton crops by the 'boll weavil' beetle.

However, after Wade Stubbs' death, Henshall Stubbs went to Grand Turk and worked the slaves in the salt ponds. Others remained behind to strike a living on their own.

Slavery was considered legal in the British territories until 1834 when the Slavery Abolition Act was finally passed by the British parliament.

'Shoulder of mutton' sail

Painting by W A Walker, 1839-1921

JANE JONES' TOMBSTONE

Below the ocean lies

Jane Jones was born in the year 1792 and was the daughter of a loyalist settler by the name of John Jones.

His wife Elizabeth was slowly adjusting to a new way of life on Salt Cay in the Turks islands, far from her working farm in Pennsylvania and its small Welsh community.

When the American Revolutionary War ended in 1783, John would not swear to the Oath of Allegiance, renouncing the authority of King George III.

Thus, John and his family decided to flee the country. With promises of a land grant and cash from the British Government, he purchased their passage to the salt islands and a new way of life in the West Indies.

As a young girl, Jane would sit outside their thatched house and listen to her pa recount stories of the Revolutionary War and how it all began in 1775.

He explained how Great Britain had fought a series of battles with thirteen of its North American colonies. Colonies that had finally won the war and declared themselves the independent United States of America.

"It all started when the British Government decided to impose high duties on sugar and tax stamps on documents, newspapers and even playing cards," her father said.

"When England lost the war," John stated, "I rightly or wrongly stayed loyal to the King and the British Empire."

Eventually John and his family settled into island life and became hard-working salt proprietors along with other settlers on the island.

In their spare time, the menfolk would fish, catch conch and turtles, build sloops or sail to nearby Grand Turk for business with other merchants.

However on 22nd August 1813, Salt Cay was struck by a terrible storm that swept across the island destroying houses, livestock and many boats.

Later it was learned that Grand Turk was practically in ruins as was the cotton plantations on the Caicos Islands.

It took a while for the Bermudian government to dispatch a schooner with vital lumber and supplies needed to help the homeless salt-rakers and merchants rebuild their homes.

By November, John Jones was still working on repairs to the house. Jane had left that morning on a sloop to Grand Turk in order to find fabric and bring home food items, a bag of rice and any other useful necessities that could be purchased from the arriving ships.

Her mother promised to sew Jane a new dress for Sunday service but secretly Jane wanted to look attractive for her soon to be fiance Joseph Seymour, who was getting ready to leave on a schooner bound for New York.

On the homeward journey from the stores in Grand Turk, a sudden gale blew up and the sloop was swamped by a raging sea. Within minutes, Jane shrieking for help was swept overboard, sunk below the ocean waves and drowned.

Joseph Seymour was devastated, and on his return voyage from New York brought with him a heavy, six foot engraved marble headstone, which was dropped in the ocean over Jane's final resting place. Today, the stone is submerged and still lies out near the White House on the West side of Salt Cay.

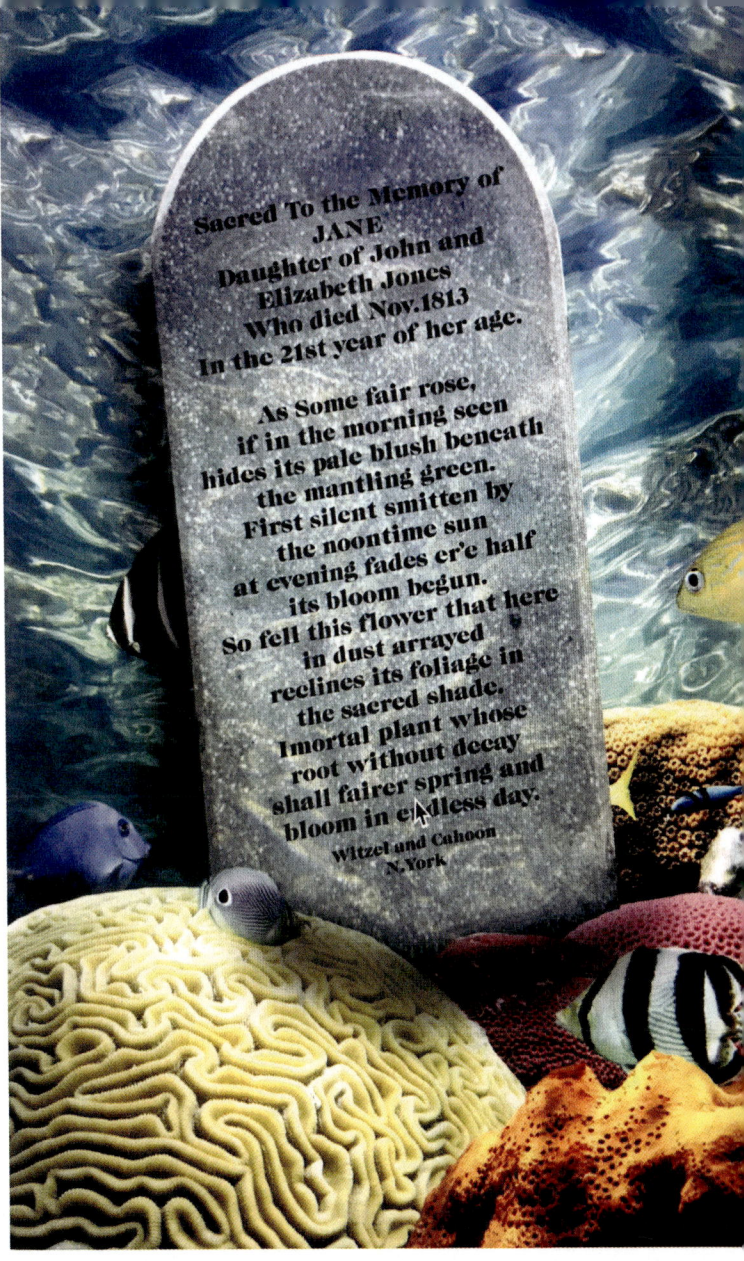

Sacred To the Memory of
JANE
Daughter of John and
Elizabeth Jones
Who died Nov.1813
In the 21st year of her age.

As Some fair rose,
if in the morning seen
hides its pale blush beneath
the mantling green.
First silent smitten by
the noontime sun
at evening fades er'e half
its bloom begun.
So fell this flower that here
in dust arrayed
reclines its foliage in
the sacred shade,
Imortal plant whose
root without decay
shall fairer spring and
bloom in endless day.
Witzel and Cahoon
N.York

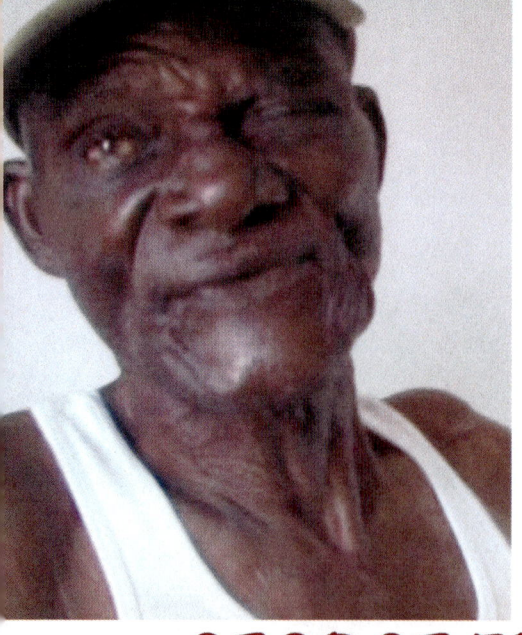

GEORGE FRANK FORBES

Sailing for Sponge on the Caicos Reefs

Historically, the salt raking Turks Islands and the arable farming Caicos Islands had a strong cultural connection that has steadily matured over centuries.

Every week or so, the Caicos sloops sailed to the Turks islands and sold their charcoal, 'ground' food, blades, palm hats and fish.

They also carried timber which was essential for building sloops and fishing boats on the more barren islands of Grand Turk and Salt Cay.

The building of boats was a skilled profession, passed down from generation to generation on each of the islands providing the means for men to make an honest living from the sea.

By the mid 1900s, salt island men were still raking salt, while the men from the Caicos islands and Providenciales were engaged in farming, conching and the sponging industries.

One such man who told me all about 'sailing for sponge' was George Frank Forbes, known fondly by all as Frank from the Byte.

He was born in 1924 in the settlement of Bottle Creek, North Caicos to father John Isaiah Forbes and mother Rebecca Ann Smith Forbes who had a small farm growing peas, corn, cassava, potato and bananas.

However, Frank spent most of his younger days at sea. "The old time people taught me how to use a compass and to read charts," he said.

"It was watching the older men, like carpenter Henry Henfield, that taught me how to build a boat."

The Elephant Ear Sponge

The Yellow Sponge

It was many years of hard work before Mr Forbes was able to build his own sturdy wooden, eight ton boat named the '*Zelma Rose*.'

The sidings were made of yellow pine and timber from the bush. The sails came from Canada and many a voyage was made to the Bahamas in his hand crafted sailing boat.

Caicos boats sailed to Nassau to sell sponge to the Greek merchants. "We couldn't land the sponge by day," said Frank; "we had to wait for nightfall so we could spread the sponge out. Then the Greeks would give us a price.

"Sometimes we would pack the sponges tightly into sweet milk boxes. The sponge was then carted to the 'Sponge Exchange' where they were sold at auction depending on their grade.

"There are grass sponge, yellow sponge, reef sponge and sheep's wool sponge," said Frank, "and you get more money for the wool sponge because it's soft and nice.

"From Bay Street to Thompson's Folly, thousands of sponges could be seen spread on water catchments, fences and rooftops where they were laid out to dry.

"The season for sponging begun in October when the larger boats sailed out to the Banks with a crew of five to seven. On arriving at the sponge grounds, two men would go in the rower to look for them.

"One man sculled over the sponge beds while the other leaned over the bow, armed with a pronged fork mounted on a twenty-five foot pole. We laid a sponge glass on the surface of the water enabling us to have a clear vision below."

The Wool Sponge

Once spotted, the sponger would thrust the primitive animal with the fork. This continued until the deck was full of sponge.

The crew would then sail back home and unload the foul-smelling sponge into a shallow water 'crawl' made out of wattle.

This enclosure permitted the tidal water and waves to wash the detritus black matter from the sponge that would later be beaten and cleaned to expose the marketable skeleton beneath.

The sponge was then dried and packed ready for the voyage to Nassau.

"Those days," said Frank, "you had to get your clearance from South Caicos, get your manifest, and then sail to Nassau in order to sell all that sponge, for peanuts.

"Believe me... I preferred my job in the office at Treasure Beach Hotel, telephone in hand... that was the easiest time of my life!"

Using a spy glass to look for Sponge in the Caicos Islands

The Sponge Exchange
&
Sponge Fleet Nassau

THE CUBAN CROW

Corvus nasicus

According to research, the Cuban crow is one of four crows that live in the Caribbean area, sharing similar characteristics with the white-necked crow found in nearby Dominican Republic and Haiti and the Jamaican crow found in the woodlands and hills of Jamaica.

The fourth crow, called the palm crow, lives in the pine forests of Haiti and the Dominican republic. It is genetically smaller in form and in appearance more closely resembles a raven or fish crow found in North America.

As the name suggests, the Cuban crow lives in most parts of Cuba, the neighbouring Island of Isla de la Juventud, parts of the Southern Bahamas and the Caicos Islands in the Turks and Caicos.

They frequent woody and forest areas and have no objection to semi-sparse woodland and agricultural areas so long as there are a muster of high trees.

The residents of North and Middle Caicos are familiar with the Cuban crows that flock to the villages. They are seen resting in trees and rummaging on the ground nipping at grain and other seeds in the yards and small holdings.

These crows have adapted well to living near people but they are often seen as a nuisance. Their distinctive cry is eardrum piercing and often described by locals as a high pitched screech, "aaaaauh"... "aaaauh"... "aaauh."

They have solid brown reddish eyes and their long, black bill has a gentle curve towards the tip. There is a patch of dark grey, bare skin behind the eyes.

The legs and feet are black as is the bluish-purple, black shine of the plumage which looks glossy in the sunlight. They are fine looking crows by all accounts.

Cuban crows are omnivorous, feeding on a variety of food of both plant and animal origin. Besides the chicken feed and odd waste scavenged from backyards their main diet is fruit, insects, spiders and geckos.

Small sea-faring critters abandoned on the shore are also happily picked over by the crows for the scrapings of meat within the shells. Gathering sticks and twigs from the bush, they build their nests high in the branches of palm trees that scatter the island.

During the mating season, the crows separate into pairs and the female lays her clutch of three to four eggs in the spring and early summer.

THE WHALING INDUSTRY IN THE TURKS ISLANDS

In the late 19th century

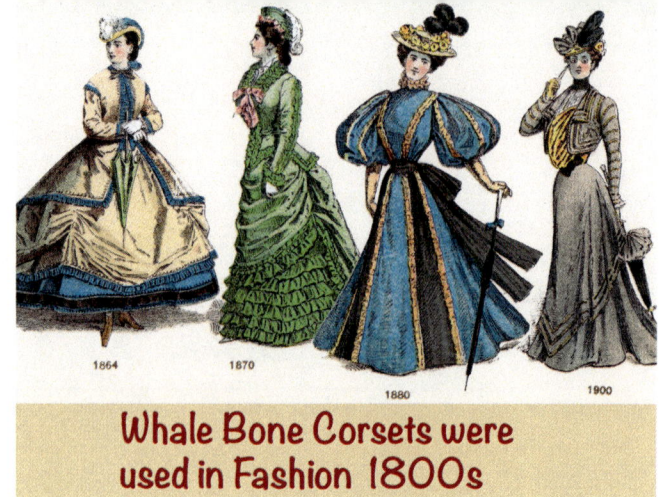

Whale Bone Corsets were used in Fashion 1800s

Earl Talbot's granddaddy Theophilus Carmichael was born in the late 1800s and was known to be a skilled pilot and fisherman and Captain of the lighter named the **Dove**, owned by the Morgan family, prominent traders in salt.

As a boy, Theophilus learned boating skills from the island mariners and listened in wonder to the stories often recounted by his father who spent many hours at sea as a whaler with the Turks Islands Whaling Company formed in 1846.

Two years previously Queen Victoria had appointed George Benvenuto Mathews as Governor of the Bahamas and while in office he encouraged the formation of the whaling industry in the Turks islands because of the increased demand for whale oil.

In England, the Industrial Revolution was in full swing and the boom in the locomotive train network meant oil was required in large quantities to lubricate the movable parts. It was also needed by the mills and factories to grease the machinery and to soften the fabric used to make boat sails.

Taylor's Hill on Salt Cay

Many more households were using oil to illuminate lamps and the whalebones were popular in women's corsets and to provide a frame for the more flamboyant dresses of the aristocracy.

Meanwhile, across the ocean on Salt Cay, the headquarters of the newly formed whaling station was located atop Taylor's Hill on the North East coast, providing a clear view of the Atlantic Ocean. From here the lookout man used a spyglass to span the horizon for 'blowers,' a name they coined for whales.

Once called to action, the crew likely to row the six man whale-boats were the tough mariners: Lightbourne, Mullins, Seymour, Talbot, Todd, Williams, Dickenson, Taylor and a man named Mr Deers who was the 'headman'.

The boat was rigged with mast, sail, rudder and oars and carried an assortment of harpoons, hatchets and lances and the essential wooden tubs spooled with 150 fathoms of strong hemp line for dragging the whale back to shore.

On board too, they secured drinking water, tobacco pipes and the essential small bucket called a 'piggin' which was necessary for bailing water from the boat during the 'frenzy of the hunt'.

Mr Deers would have stood at the stern commanding the boat as he maneuvered the steering oar. Meanwhile, four crew-men rowed the boat as the harpooner stood up front pulling the bow oar.

In fact, there is a lovely story told by the crew of the sloop *Augustus* which had left the Turks Islands for Nassau in April 1846 after having caught a whale near the Cays.

They spoke of the 'Amateur Whaling Party' from Salt Cay having also harpooned a whale off 'Pilcher's Hole' on the South side of the island.

They told the story of how the "boat's crew gave chase and soon got alongside the whale when the headman Mr Deers planted well his harpoon above the centre of the back of the animal but the harpoon being old and entirely rusty broke off."

Not to be deterred, the Salt Cay crew thrust 'sharpened irons' at the whale until it was exhausted but unfortunately in the confusion, the 50 fathoms of line broke.

Without hesitation, one brave man, possibly Talbot, dived under the whale for the end of the rope and rejoined the line.

It was not long before a number of boats arrived with bayonets and other weapons and plunged them into the blubber, which finally killed the whale.

By nightfall they had heaved the whale to shore ready to be peeled, sliced, minced and boiled in the whale pots producing 17 or 18 barrels of oil for the market.

LEWIS TEMPLE

And the Toggle Head Iron Harpoon...

Throughout the 1800s men set sail on long voyages to hunt whales for their meat, oil and blubber. Baleen found in a whale's jaw was used to make fishing line, shape ladies stays and weave baskets.

However, it was a man called Lewis Temple who invented a particular head for the harpoon called a 'Temples' toggle or 'Temples' iron.

It became the standard harpoon of the whaling trade industry in the middle of the nineteenth century.

Temple had been born into slavery in 1800 and for many years worked as a plantation labourer in Richmond, Virginia.

In 1836, he became a free black man and before long and through sheer determination became a skilled blacksmith and a successful business man. He opened a whaling shop on the New Bedford Waterfront in Massachusetts which was then known as the principal seaport for whaling.

The whalers bought the Toggle head because of its movable head which when thrust at the whale locked deep in the flesh which helped prevent the whale from escaping.

It is quite likely that the harpooners in Grand Turk and Salt Cay would have used these harpoons or something similar.

A contributing factor to the rapid decline of the whaling industry in 1859 was the discovery of mineral oil in Pennsylvania.

This led to the reduced demand for whale oil lamps and spermaceti candles.

However by the late 1800s the whaling industry had tapered off. Many ships had been lost during the American Civil War and entrepreneurs turned their attention to other commodities like cotton and sisal.

By the year 1888 and with the death of the overseer Mr James Wilson, the Salt Cay Whaling Company closed its doors and all that remains today is a whaling pot and the broken-down stone wall tank in which the oil was stored.

The 'Toggle Head' harpoon invented in 1848 by Lewis Temple revolutionized the whaling industry.

Whaling in the 18th Century
Painting by Nina Shilling

Great Earthquake Disaster. Royal Mail Booking Office, Kingston, Jamaica, W.I.

A STORY OF THE DEVASTATING JAMAICAN EARTHQUAKE 1907

Monday, January 14, 1907, 3.30pm, Local Time

For all intents and purposes, Kingston the Capital of Jamaica was the usual bright sunny day and the streets were alive with the hustle and bustle of commerce, off-duty sailors, fruit and basket sellers, strollers and window shoppers. A typical Monday afternoon.

The time was roughly 3.30pm on that fateful day, when out of nowhere was heard a terrible rushing and roaring of wind filled with a violent shaking, weaving and rolling of the ground that was shocking to witness.

Within minutes the town was enveloped in a fog of thick, white dust. Many of the buildings had collapsed and the streets were dense with rubble, debris and scattered bodies of the dead and dying. The panic was palpable and the moaning and shrieks of anguish were heard on every street corner.

Kingston had been destroyed in a couple of minutes and before anyone could mobilize into any form of rescue operation, a series of fierce fires broke out and swept through the City adding to the confusion and a higher death toll.

Commercial buildings and the important warehouses that stored the daily exports were burnt to a cinder and brought commerce to a stop.

Finally, it was logged that more than eight hundred people had died in the earthquake and over 10,000 residents had been left homeless and stranded in a broken city.

The Kingston earthquake registered a magnitude of 6.5 and later, as news spread around the globe, became known as one of the world's deadliest earthquakes.

One of the Elder, Dempster & Co passenger steamships that moored in Kingston harbour during the 1907 earthquake was the **SS Port Kingston.** She was there to have repairs carried out on the ship when suddenly the blast from the earthquake shook the steamer.

According to one eye witness account, the whole city "rocked like a ship in a choppy sea and entire streets were leveled to the ground" and "when the fire broke out on King Street, the flames engulfed and fried the people in it's wake."

Traveling on board the **Port Kingston** was an industrious businessman by the name of Sir Alfred Lewis Jones, renowned for his shipping acumen and for his help in creating the important Liverpool School of Tropical Medicine that researched diseases like sleeping sickness.

She was there to have some repairs carried out on the ship when suddenly the blast from the earthquake shook the steamer.

Now, Sir Jones, originally from Wales, was invited by Joseph Chamberlain, then Secretary for the Colonies, to help develop trade with the West Indies. This trip to Jamaica with his colleagues was to seek new ventures in the West Indies pertaining to the cotton trade.

Sir Alfred Lewis Jones

It so happened that Jones was also the new owner of the **Port Kingston**, and had established the Imperial Direct West India Mail Service Co to run between Jamaica and Bristol, arranging with one of his firms, Elders and Fyffes, to import bananas into Britain.

In fact Sir Jones made a valiant attempt to stimulate the Jamaican fruit trade and tourist industry in Jamaica.

And so it was, when the earthquake struck on that fateful afternoon, there were many casualties and Sir Jones leapt into action turning the **Port Kingston** into a floating hospital with makeshift operating rooms.

It is said that over two hundred people crowded the decks with various injuries and the ship's doctor, Arthur Evans, nurse Cross and others worked around the clock to save lives.

If the **Port Kingston** could talk, it would tell stories of the many wealthy tourists and of the passengers from the Turks and Caicos who were traveling back and forth to Jamaica for business.

50

Stories told by Bishop Wilfred Hornby of Nassau, Sydney, Haldene Olivier, Governor of Jamaica and the current Commissioner of the Turks and Caicos, Mr Frederick Henry Watkins.

All of these characters had an important part to play in the early 1900s social and economic life. Two years after the death of Sir Jones in 1909, the ship was converted into a troop ship for use during the great war.

Unfortunately she sank in 1930 when her propeller shaft snapped four hundred miles off Raratonga in the Cook islands, tearing a large hole in her stern.

All passengers were rescued and lived to tell more fascinating stories of their own.

The once lively **SS Port Kingston** lies on the ocean floor ending an important chapter in history.

SS Port Kingston on its way to Jamaica

MEANWHILE IN GRAND TURK

The Frith family, prominent merchants and brokers of salt and other commodities were going about their business checking on the salt yield from the ponds, and the comings and goings along Front Street where they had a large store. A sign on the wall announced 'Frith Brothers & Co. Salt Manufacturers.'

The store faced the ocean and was within easy walking distance of the bustling dock where men and women were seen every day engaged in a multitude of activities. The steam boats arrived with their passengers, cargo and mail while the sloops and lighters went back and forth with salt and often decks full of fish, fruit and coal delivered from the Caicos islands.

The Frith family lived in Palm Grove at the time, and on hearing the news from Kingston were most upset. Below is part of a letter written to friends about the Kingston earthquake.

> ### Palm Grove
> ### Turks Islands
> ### 1907
>
> I have written to the Campbells, Rocks, Morrisons and others but do not know if they are dead or alive. 1200 persons were killed so it is supposed. 500 were recognized, 353 were buried one afternoon, 20 at a time in deep graves, 343 on another day.
>
> All put in, indiscriminately, no time for coffins. Now they burn the bodies as they find them under the removed ruins. I do hope the Hardwicks are safe. For 24 hours, not a drop of water could be got in Hampton and the fire raging and the tropical sun beating down.
>
> It must have been something awful. A party of tourists from Bristol left Saturday afternoon. When they get here tomorrow there is a terrible surprise waiting for them... poor things!

> We had a memorial services all day Sunday and a public meeting on the parade Sunday afternoon at 5 o' clock held by the commissioner.
>
> Mr Sampson read prayers. Mr Stocky read the 90th psalm. Mr Pusey spoke "for the voice of the Lord is not in the wind, nor in the earthquake, nor in the fire. Trust in the still, small, voice." We sang My God and Father, Brief Life and Rock of Ages.
>
> Winnie played on a small harmonium, there were about 600 out, Mr and Mrs Watkins, 3 Howells, Pa Geoffrey Been and I. L and A D Ted and Connie, Smiths, Harriotts and Jones, Darrells, Samsons etc.
>
> Mr Pusey is gone I expect in Hampton. Mr Shelby's people are safe in Montego Bay, he goes to Jamaica tomorrow and returns the end of March. He will offer his services to the injured and dying ones. The Bela does not go into Bermuda this trip but on to Jamaica. Stanley Jones goes down on her...

Ever since the first telegraph cable was laid in 1898 providing a link between Jamaica, Bermuda and Grand Turk, communication had improved and news between the islands could be sent quickly by telegram.

Thus it was that within hours of the Kingston earthquake all the gentry and most of the town-folk in Grand Turk had heard of the tragedy.

The Post Master, Commissioner, Friths, Jones and Hinsons would have heard first of the terrible news from Jamaica.

During the turn of the century all these men were key players in society life and played an important role in the rise and fall of the economy.

They shared a strong network of friends which reached both near and far including family members and colleagues working or settled in Jamaica.

The Frith family was no exception, and as a well-known local family had many business connections and friends in both Kingston and Montego Bay.

Besides the export of salt, the Friths managed the West Caicos Fibre Company for a few years, planting over 1500 acres with sisal. This venture provided work for islanders from nearby islands.

From their two-storey house in Palm Grove, the Friths enjoyed entertaining the Grand Turk dignitaries including William D. Young from British Columbia who became the colonial administrator of the Turks Islands from 1901 until 1905.

They discussed the possibility of a boat and steamship service for the islands which resulted in the approval of a 'port of call' at Grand Turk with an en-route service from England to Jamaica.

The Imperial Direct West India Mail Service Co. was registered in 1901 and the steamers were soon arriving to Grand Turk with cargo, passengers and mail.

It was the era of Queen Victoria's reign of global expansion of the British Empire and rapid advances in industry, science and communications. Thus, the economic and social life in Grand Turk during the 18th and early 19th centuries were heavily influenced by her long reign which spanned six decades.

When she died in January 1901, her eldest son King Edward VII succeeded to the throne ending the Victorian era and marking a brief phase in history referred to as the Edwardian Period.

THE IMPERIAL DIRECT WEST INDIA MAIL SERVICE Co LTD

"ARRIVAL OF AN IMPERIAL DIRECT WEST INDIA MAIL STEAMER AT THE WEST INDIES"

REGULAR FORTNIGHTLY SAILINGS TO AND FROM JAMAICA AND AVONMOUTH (BRISTOL) ALSO TO BERMUDA EVERY SIX WEEKS

ELDER, DEMPSTER & Co COLONIAL HOUSE, LIVERPOOL. & AT CANADA HOUSE. BRISTOL. 4. ST.MARY AXE. LONDON.E.C. 30. MOSLEY ST. MANCHESTER. CARDIFF. HAMBURG. ETC.

Queen Victoria

MS ONA GLINTON

One of Grand Turk's well-loved educators of the 20th century

This incredible lady from Grand Turk, Ms Ona Glinton was a wealth of knowledge and wisdom. A very special lady born on June 13th 1910 and lived to be over 100 years old. She was a well-known educator and the local school on Grand Turk was named after her.

Her father was a master pilot in Grand Turk just like her grandfather, guiding the boats and ships in and out of the town dock in Grand Turk.

Ms Ona was raised by her godfather Richard Been from Salt Cay who at the time was a government officer. He sent her to the Cecil Earl Crawford School which back then cost 10 shillings a month to attend. In fact, one of her first teachers was Ms Iris Adams, a local lady who was schooled in Jamaica.

Her mother too, was a teacher and strict disciplinarian and was born in the late 1800s when Queen Victoria was still on the throne. Her name was Angelina Lightbourne, and Ms Ona recalls that her mother was a small, bright-skinned woman, a good seamstress, musician and a singer in the Methodist Church.

In 1946, Ms Ona was married to a Salt Cay man by the name of Wilfred Glinton. He was a sailor that worked on the Dutch ships but one day he fell sick with a cold that developed into pneumonia and he died at sea. They had two loving children, Frederick and Hyacinth.

During her mother's years, William Douglas Young was the colonial administrator. He arrived in Grand Turk in 1901 and was instrumental in introducing the Island's first currency note and enabled the construction of the Victoria public buildings on Front Street, which housed the legislature.

Now, during Commissioner Young's time in office, the Elder. D. Steamship Company was inaugurated in 1905, and steamships, called 'banana boats,' would stop in Grand Turk on their way to Bermuda and Jamaica from England.

This was just another avenue of transporting people, cargo, mail and of course news from England and Europe.

Meanwhile the flagship for the island was a 23 ton ship named the *President*, which sailed between the Islands and was often chartered by the Government for official business. She was launched in 1850 from the island of Salt Cay.

When Ms Ona Glinton was born in 1910, Grand Turk wharf and dock was a busy port of entry. Thousands of bushels of salt would leave these shores and many sloops from the Caicos islands would arrive to Grand Turk with their home-grown produce.

The locals went about their daily lives fishing, farming, sailing, building boats, baking bread and homemaking.

Their lives were tough, and the necessity to work and make money to feed the family meant many adults had a limited education or could not afford the fees.

It is certainly true that in prior years and before the abolition of slavery, only the church and missionaries made any effort to school children.

It was when Alexander Forth became President of the Turks Islands in 1848 that formal education began to be taken more seriously.

He believed children should have access to education and set up an Education Board to monitor and create education policies for all the islands.

Consequently more schools were built in the Salt Islands and the Caicos townships.

Decades later in the post war years, and during the Jamaican administration, a select number of islanders like Raymond Gardener, Ms Ona Glinton, Mary Robinson and her sister Helena went for teacher training at the Mico Teaching College in Kingston, Jamaica.

By the early 1900s, the Mico College was considered the best teacher training college in the West Indies and men and women from the Turks and Caicos were encouraged to sail to Jamaica for their training.

Many older folk may have heard of other educators who attended the college, like R. G. Wint and Father Clifford Jones.

Mica training College in Jamaica

Originally the college was founded by the British abolitionist and social reformer Sir Thomas Fowell Buxton, who advocated that after the Abolition of Slavery Act 1833, the freed enslaved should be entitled to an education.

Not long after this declaration, Buxton instigated the building of a school through the Lady Mico Trust fund which led to the formation of a network of boys and girls schools for indigenous students and a praiseworthy school system in the Caribbean.

Abolitionist
Sir Thomas
Buxton

The Mica
Training
College

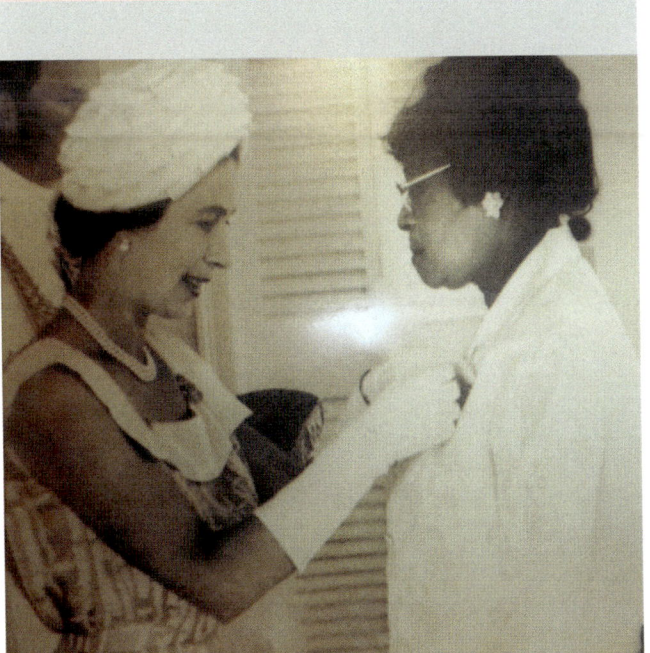

Queen Elizabeth II, honours
educator Helena Robinson

Cannon Jones and his wife Mary
Astwood presented to the Queen
Elizabeth II and Prince Philip

Certainly Ms Ona Glinton remembers
her former teacher, Mr R. G. Wint, who in
actual fact taught her mother and
served for 31 years in the Turks islands.

Ms Ona recalls when Mr J. D. Wood was
the principal of the Salt Cay school on
Victoria Street, long before the school
was named Mary Robinson. He too was
trained in Jamaica.

55

"My family all hailed from men of the
sea. They loved the sea. One of the
principal jobs was guiding the ships to a
safe anchorage... vessels arriving from
foreign lands, coming to collect the salt.

"Every ship needed a pilot to bring them
closer to shore. It was dangerous work
and one of my grandfathers drowned in
what must have been a storm.

"My father was Mary Lightbourne's son
named John and he was from Salt Cay.
He also was a pilot but there were many
of them back then. All wanted to be
employed. If there was a schooner to
Westward they would rush with their pilot
boats to be chosen to bring the ships to
safety.

"To feed the family, my father used to go night fishing for fish and conch. Next morning you might find a nice big snapper outside your door. We were happy to find that fish, we knew we would have fried fish and rice next day.

"We grew our own Indian corn in our yard. They were hard times in those days but everyone tried to help each other.

"When I was young my mother Angelina Lightbourne could not keep me. I know I was her favourite, she told me so, but I had to live with other members of the family. I would stay with my grand-mummy 'over-back' and sometimes with Mary in Salt Cay. She was a seamstress and a homemaker, a lovely set of people.

"Uncle Freddy Simmons was family on Salt Cay and I remember the Morgans. There was Susy and her son James Morgan.

"The man who raised me though was a Salt Cay man by the name of Richard Been. He was my Godfather. It was God's will that he took care of me. You may have heard of him, you hear his name all about, 'RB'. He had three wives... as one wife died he married again.

"They were important merchants and pond owners but they were always nice to people.

"Richard was a tailor, the best tailor on the island. People came from away to have their clothes made by him. He had the big two-storey house on Salt Cay.

"I ate there, slept there and anything I needed, he provided for me even though there were plenty of children in the house. He was in the government service, must be all his life... a very kind and friendly man that sent me to the 'Cecil, Earl Crawford School.'

"He came from Barbados. We had to pay fees and back then it was ten shillings a month. We also had our school uniforms and books to pay for.

"When Mr Crawford held prize givings, the service was in the Anglican Church and we all showed up in our uniforms and with our families present. We had a lovely time and after the service finished we held a big party with food and soda.

"My very first teacher though was Iris Adams. Her father was Christy Adams, a strong member of the Methodist.

"Well, Ms Adams was trained at Mica Jamaica and I had some of her schooling when she came home.

"We learnt so many things at school. I never thought I was smart but I was very thankful to my godfather that he took an interest in my education.

"My father could not do that for me because he did not have money to pay for uniforms and so much of books piled up in your arms. I could never grumble, whatever the school called for, I had.

"My mother was a teacher, a strict disciplinarian. People called her Aunt NeeNee. She kept a school in her home, and she was glad when I left school so that I could help her. I was her daughter so I was supposed to help.

"My mother taught me crochet. The first foundation of crochet was chains, treble and half treble. As I went on, I learned better things. When I was a good size and could read, I followed the patterns in the books to see how things were done.

"At about the same time there was another good natured white woman who was the wife of B.C. Frith and her name was Ms Virginia Sawyer from America.

"She was the second wife of B.C. Frith and was twenty years younger and they lived up in the big house in Palm Grove.

"She was a very kind and generous lady. She taught me and many young girls the art of fine needlework and crochet.

"Any girl who was interested in crochet or sewing, she would help. All you had to do was go up to her door.

"She had two servants by the name of Minora Williams and Ms Jessie Wint. She had those girls like her daughters.

Crossed Triple Crochet Stitch

Frances Streeter first wife of B.C Frith Died November 1910

58

"When she went to America about her business those girls could go up to the house and eat and do what they liked, sleep there and all. Her husband, B. C. Frith often had business in New York which enabled Mrs Frith to take orders and sell the crochet work in America. We would crochet all kind of things and what we didn't know she would teach us.

"When our crochet was sold, she would bring the money to us girls. We would make big bedspreads... Bless these fingers, they were good.

"My mother also worked up in the house with B.C. Frith's mother Mrs Jane Butterfield, (1827-1910). She died four weeks after B.C. Frith's wife passed.

"Ma did the washing, cleaning and helped with the cooking. She was wonderful, not because she was my mother... she was just a wonderful person. She loved the Methodist Church and loved music.

"When she was younger, she was taken in by Mr Wint and his wife. They loved my mother like nothing.

Virginia Sawyer Frith, the second wife of B.C. Frith

Palm Grove
Grand Turk

"In those days family and friends helped each other out so my grandmother Sarah Been let my mother live with the Wints.

"Grandfather was a seaman and used to sail from Grand Turk to Puerto Plata and back bringing freight, fruit and things. They used to call him 'Baggy Been.'

"Another crochet maker I remember was Ethel Lightbourne, and there was also a dark woman by the name of Ethlyn Been. She was married to a Colbrooke and after day-school my mother would send me to her. I was her scholar, but she could not teach me much as my mother was the best at crochet and had taught me all the stitches.

"Now I can tell you my ma could dance and I liked to dance. Salt Cay people like to dance and the men like to play the mouth organ and the ripsaw... anything they could get their hands on, like pots and pans. These old legs could dance and I used to like what we called 'kadrills'.

"Serenading at Christmas and every year we would dance at the junkanoo. My family played music. Rosie on Salt Cay is my family. She loved to sew and play the piano and amuse everyone in the 'entertainment' program.

"My ma showed me how to use plants for when you got the colds and which bush weeds to boil to make tea for coughs. In my time I had my dose. Sometimes it was slimy like nothing else, but you have got to drink it. You put a little salt in it and you will be cured.

"If I have a message to everyone, it is to be kind. If anyone wants to help you, and you know they are capable of doing so, appreciate it. Trust in God because He knows everything. Go down on your knees and pray. He hears and will help you through your deepest troubles!

"My favourite hymn is 'How Great Thou Art,' which was also the favorite song of my mother who loved to sing this in the Grand Turk Methodist Church."

How Great Thou Art

O LORD my God! When I in awesome wonder
Consider all the works Thy hand hath made;
I see the stars, I hear the mighty thunder,
Thy pow'r throughout the universe displayed:

Then sings my soul, my Saviour God, to Thee,
How great Thou art! How great Thou art!
Then sings my soul, my Saviour God, to Thee,
How great Thou art! How great Thou art!

When through the woods and forest glades I wander
And hear the birds sing sweetly in the trees;
When I look down from lofty mountain grandeur,
And hear the brook, and feel the gentle breeze:

And when I think that God, His Son not sparing,
Sent Him to die - I scarce can take it in:
That on the Cross, my burden gladly bearing,
He bled and died to take away my sin:

When Christ shall come with shout of acclamation
And take me home - what joy shall fill my heart!
Then shall I bow in humble adoration,
And there proclaim, my God how great Thou art!

VICTORIAN MORALS AND MANNERS ON THE ISLANDS

There were a few 'grand dames' living on Salt Cay who were best friends for well over seventy years. Together, they witnessed many life-changing events on the island including the move from oil lamps to electricity.

From a sociological point of view these older folk, in their youth, lived through an era when community adhered to a strict code of ethics. The eldest of these remarkable ladies was Ms Melvina Simmons who we fondly called Ms Melly.

She could recount stories of days growing up on Salt Cay during the 20th century, when chores had to be completed, devotions said daily and children obeyed or risked the wrath of a good whipping.

These oral stories give us an inkling of how community life functioned in the Turks and Caicos islands long after the death of Queen Victoria.

Ms Melly describes her mother, Ms Emily Eliza Kennedy as a strict, hard women with a 'no messing about' attitude ... "if you did not jump to attention you'd be pinched or whipped."

This strictness was indicative of the 1900s and Victorian morality which had spread throughout the Empire leaving behind a strict code of values: loyalty, hard work, respectability, punctual attendance at church and obedience.

Evangelicals and missionaries preached good moral conduct and the importance of female chastity. Girls were therefore closely watched especially at dances.

The young men arrived in black pants and 'dickies' while the women wore long sweepers. They danced under lamplight. Any act of impropriety and the girls were marched home for a good beating.

Miss Melly tells the story of when she was young and her mother and grandma, Melvina Kennedy would go fishing. By the time they reached home somewhere after noon, the children were expected to have completed all the chores with food expected to be ready for the table. You had to mind your P's and Q's. It was a 'no nonsense' household ruled by her father Roderick Robinson, an intelligent man.

"There was nothing he couldn't do," said Melly, "he was a mason and he kept pigs, donkeys, mules and cows and moved houses from South to North on large rolling wheels with the men pushing and shoving." In those days, wooden houses were often relocated when couples intended marriage.

Certainly entrepreneurial, Roderick was also the agent for the turtle catchers from Nassau, bringing in their catch to the town dock to be sold. With many mouths to feed Roderick spent hours making shoes as a cobbler and had his own set of tools including an anvil, hammers, stick for measuring and stretching pliers for the leather.

Roderick too, was a salt raker who had his own shares in the pond. "He made us children put on our shoes, early in the morning, and go and rake salt," laughed Ms Melly, "and then we got it ready for the next morning when the mule and cart would carry it out, and all of this before sunrise when he went to his day work."

Ms Melly's stories help demonstrate that in the late 1800s onwards community life on Salt Cay centered on good Victorian morals and manners, hard work and discipline. Obey or get a good licking was the order of the day!

MS MELVINA SIMMONS FROM SALT CAY

"I was born in Salt Cay. My father was Roderick James Robinson and my mother was Emily Elisa Kennedy Robinson.

My father was a very intelligent man. There was nothing that my father couldn't do. He was a mason and a man that moved wooden houses from South to North on wheels.

"Sometimes they would break down and you had to stop and fix the cart back up again and when you say 'halt, halt, halt'... you got to heave things into place. There used to be plenty men pushing those houses.

"When the wheel break, the men had to all stand to one side while the wheel get fixed and then you would start pushing the house all over again. 'Hup, hup, hup, let's go,' you would hear my father say. They gone and boy, that house be spinning.

"Now my father were a South man, and married to my mother a North woman. When he wanted to take his house North, he gathered the men together and they took his house from Eastward of Maurice Simmons, and carried it way down to the North of Jack's house.

"He had a yard in which were kept horses, cows, mules and donkeys. He was really a local entrepreneur and did many things... mason, move houses, keep animals, sell turtles and he used to sit down and make his little shoes to wear.

"My parents were the age of eighteen when they got married and produced ten children, eight girls, two boys, me, Rosey, Ella, Leonie, Joyce (dead), Susie (dead), Sarah (dead), Louis (dead), brother James (dead).

"My Ma was a very strict woman and a hard woman too... you got to look like you doing what she say. If you don't do what she say, she is going to pinch you hard. Oh yes, she was a hard woman but she had a soft side too.

"We would always get ready for Christmas and do a lot of hard work. You gotta paint and plaster and you have to look like you are working hard while my mother sitting down.

"Ma would go and collect the wood and sometimes of a morning she would go fishing with her mother on the Bay. Her mother's name was Ms Melvina Kennedy and I'm named after her.

"They would return in the afternoon around one or three carrying the fish. Now us children have to have the house cleaned and the food done cooked before they reach.

"We would be cooking fish mostly but we used to get a lot of turtle in those days. Oh yes, the turtlers used to come here and my father was the agent for them and would sell them to all his customers.

"The turtlers would go out in their boats. They would come to these waters from Nassau and catch all the turtles. Turtle was very cheap back then and in great demand ... not what it's like now.

"There were plenty of turtles in those days.

"The turtlers came to town weekends and would have all their turtles ready cut up and then my pa would dispose of the meat to the families.

"Now the way to fix a turtle is to take all the hard back off the meat and then you steam it down to make a very nice soup. Throw in your addles, whatever you have to hand and give it a good seasoning.

"My pa like I said ever worked in the salt pans... always a hard worker. Same thing when he built houses. The children had to be up there and look like they are mixing mortar. All us girls had to learn how to mix mortar and do it well. If pa was doing carpentry and measuring a piece of wood, he would say, 'cut that and I mean cut it straight' and we had to look like we cutting it straight and then pass the wood to him to fix up high.

"Come teenager, you couldn't get in love with no boys... ma had to pick for you. They were very strict.

Credit to Artist Winslow Homer 1899

63

"Now Will had loved me a long time but it was hard to decide if I wanted him. When I finally decided to love him, I told him that if he don't mean it, don't start it. I never had it in my mind to go down, I wanted to go up. He got in love with me in October and by December we were engaged for two years.

"I were a girl who went to school with Lyla Bassett. She was married to a man by the name of Mr L. Bassett who was doing his salt work loading the Steamers, working on the boats and helping those boatmen that came up from the Caicos selling their coal and feed for the animals.

"At the dock you would see the salt bags were on one side and the Caicos boats were moored on the other side to unload their goods.

"Anyway, at the same time that me and Will were talking nuptials, Lyla's husband died. Soon after, Lyla was planning to remove to Grand Turk to be near her brothers and sisters.

"One day after her sewing class I told her I wanted to get married but I couldn't see a home and asked her if she would mind selling the little house by the gate.

"She said she would but wondered how it could be moved... that's when my pa agreed to help. With his friends, they took away the stones and hauled the wooden house up onto the rollers of a cart and took it South. It took two days!

The House of Lyla Bassett in the Distance

Salt raking on Salt Cay

"Let me speak of Christmas again. In our household, we had very little of anything... not like now. Getting ready for Christmas you didn't do the painting the same way as today. We would make up a paste and put a little 'aloes' in it and that's what we used.

"Right up to Christmas morning looks like, you were pasting those partitions to make them look nice. 'Cleanliness is next to Godliness,' must be.

"And when you're talking about Christmas Eve night, well let me tell you, children aren't like today, back then they wouldn't even go out the house... Too afraid of Santa Claus... What!

"We would be baking our bread and our cakes for the morrow and getting the wood from the bush to heat the oven.

"We would rake up all them little coals and put our bread and little cakes up on top. You had to keep watching. We knew nothing about those box ovens like you have today.

"They smelt very beautiful and taste very nice... oh yes! And wine, my father used to make his own wine and put it in the sun for so many days. You bury the wine in the ground and take it out Christmas week and sweeten it up... now that's the wine we used to have.

"And then you would make your beer. Remember to put a little ginger and a little corn and other little things in it.

"You've got to get the berries off the tree to make the wine, then you get your pear-buds and squeeze them, strain them off and this will fix your wine nice and good.

That was life in those days!"

STORIES OF NORMAN TALBOT

Legendary fisherman of Salt Cay

During the war many torpedo boats roamed the waters around Salt Cay and Grand Turk, and any sightings had to be reported to the Commissioner of the island or the police for documenting.

Anyway, one day Mr Norman Talbot, as was pretty normal, decided to go fishing with his friends James Smith and Luceta Kennedy. The date, to be remembered later, was August 20th 1942.

They left Dean's Dock around 6.30pm and five minutes later found themselves in the fishing grounds opposite the lighthouse. All went well until 11pm when they heard a strange sound coming from the South West and saw an object speeding across the surface of the water. The sound was coming closer and closer and all three men were becoming agitated and wanted to return to the safety of the shore.

On reaching the harbour, Luceta and James were not comfortable with continuing their fishing trip and happily went home. However, Norman could not be stopped. He headed for his shop by the beach to take another look out to sea in the direction of the fishing grounds and the unusual sound that could have been a large motor roaring across the ocean.

Lighthouse on Salt Cay

During World War II, it is claimed that the Turks and Caicos partially funded the Royal Navy frigate HMS Caicos, which was a patrol boat and an aircraft detection frigate used in the North Sea to detect German V-1 flying bombs aimed at London.

As part of the war effort many of the island women folk wove mittens and other articles for the soldiers.

Norman Talbot

He saw a hull moving very fast going South and in accordance with wartime protocol, he decided it was best to report matters to the local policeman.

"I went to look for constable Kennedy and together we went back to Dean's Dock but by then it was too late and we saw nothing.

"But in my opinion," continued Norman Talbot, "I believe the sound was coming from a German submarine. It's never a dull day on Salt Cay!"

Dean's Dock, Salt Cay

BONEFISHING IN THE ISLANDS

Thrill of the chase

Bonefish are quite remarkable and their scientific name is *Albula vulpes,* which means white fox. Another name they go by is Gray Ghosts of the Atlantic, probably because they are cunning, elusive and some of the strongest, fast-moving swimmers of salt water fish, especially when hooked.

They are named bonefish because of the number of tiny little bones in their body. There are so many of them that eating bonefish is not easy except for islanders who enjoy the whole mechanics of eating round the bones... an acquired taste.

Most anglers though enjoy the thrill of the chase and hunt bonefish on a catch-and-release basis from aboard a skiff, or wading through the tidal flats. Around the islands there are some great hunting grounds, Providenciales, the Caicos islands, Grand Turk and in the South Creek on Salt Cay.

These fish are graceful swimmers and inhabit shallow creeks, inter-tidal flats and mangrove canals in tropical and warm temperate waters worldwide. This is an important reason why bonefish are well suited for the coastal ecosystems of the Turks and Caicos.

Often the waters in the mudflats and shallow creeks are oxygen-depleted but the bonefish have a remarkable method of supplementing oxygen supply in water, by inhaling air into a lung-like bladder.

Another feature of the bonefish is the manner in which they hunt for food. They do not have teeth on show, but crush their prey with pharyngeal teeth located at the base of the throat.

They move and hunt in shoals, although some of the larger ones swim alone or in pairs. They hunt near ledges, sea-grass beds and along the sea floor, feeding on shrimps, small crabs, mollusks, little fish and worms.

First, they shuffle and seek out food along the muddy bottom of the sea with their elongated snout, filling their mouths with water and blowing the critters out of the sand and mud.

Next, the bonefish hold their catch in their strong jaw and grind their catch into pulp before swallowing. It is little wonder that bonefish can grow to almost three feet long and weigh over four pounds, making them a strong fighting fish for anglers.

For the most part, bonefish are silver in colour with a darker shade on their backs of a lightish olive colour. Soft dotted lines of grey run vertical from their gills to the tail.

To the uninitiated, bonefish resemble giant sardines!

GEORGE STEVENSON GRANT FROM BLUE HILLS

"Conching was a hard way of life"

"My name is George Stevenson Grant and I was born in Blue Hills in the year 1934. My ma was Constance Grant and when I was growing up, she worked farm way over back, far from here and they used to have a road that she walked every day to get there. She would grow peas, corn, cassava and anything you could grow.

"My pa was Cornelius Grant and he was a fisherman and when he was young he would go out sponging on the boats. My parents sent me to school but when I reached a certain age I left school to work with him.

We would go westwards to look for conch on the conching grounds. We would be a couple of men to a dinghy and you had to scull the boat with a long wooden oar to get above the conchs. Some men would dive down on them.

"When you spotted the conch by what we call a spy glass, you would hook it up with a pronged stick...a blacksmith could make them in Blue Hills... he would bend the end into a hook like and that would help lift the conch into the boat.

"We would carry on hooking conch all day... at a certain time they are all about in the banks, and in shallow water where there's plenty of sea grass. We would all work together and at sundown rest up and sing to pass time.

Using a spyglass to look for conch on the ocean bed

Drying Da Conch

"Conching was a hard way of life. We had to catch them, knock the conch out, bruise them and hang them up to let them dry. Sometimes they would be all about the yard... we had to be watchful that none went missing in the night.

"Our intention was to take them to Haiti to sell. First you had to leave from here early in the morning and sail to South Caicos where we had to clear customs or 'clear out' as it was called... that's how it was back then.

"After you finished with South Caicos you would sail round to French Cay and from there leave for Haiti and go along the coast to Port de Paix where the Captain would sell the conch to the agency."

Ebanezer Baptist Church, Sandy Point, North Caicos

MR DANIEL CAMPBELL

From Sandy Point, North Caicos

The Great World War had ended on November 11th, 1918 when Germany formally surrendered to the allied forces. Meanwhile in the Turks and Caicos Islands, George Whitfield Smith was the appointed Commissioner (1914-1923).

It was during this time that Daniel Campbell was born in the remote village of Sandy Point in North Caicos.

"I was born in 1921, and when I knew myself my father was Robert Lorenzo Campbell and my mother Letitia Louise Forbes. Although I was born in Sandy Point, my mother was from Bottle Creek.

"As a babe I lived with my grandmother in Bottle Creek, and I stayed with her for nine years. My grandmother on my mother's side was Elizabeth Henfield.

"I remember her well as a loving grandmother. As a baby, every night before the sun set, I would lay in her lap and go to sleep. I have very good memories of her.

"After her death, I was returned to my mother who was living in Sandy Point and I am still living here today.

"I never knew my father until I returned home, that's when I got to know him. To be truthful he was not educated but he was a hard working man, farming and 'fishning' (fishing) to make a living.

"He was a very religious man in the Baptist Church just along the road from here. You will be surprised to know that a part of that Church is over 150 years old.

"If you notice, the Church is shaped like a T, but the Western side where you see that bell staring at you, well that's the old part. The Church was built by my great-grandfather.

"My grandmother on my father's side was Francis Campbell. When I knew her, she was blind and couldn't see. I remember that my father and us children would carry her breakfast every morning and when evening came, we prepared her food and took it to her.

"The first school that I went to was a walk away in Bottle Creek and my teacher was Coral Alberta Seymour. She use to be called head teacher in our day, and assistant teachers were called monitors. There were many of them and some I can recall. There was Gillsie Faym Gardener, Paulette Seymour and Ms Emily Taylor.

"Back in the days they used to teach sums, different types of arithmetic, reading and writing but always in the morning we had what you call devotions and would sing Psalm 92:-

"It is a good thing to give thanks unto the Lord, and to sing praises unto thy name, O Most High:

"To shew forth thy loving kindness in the morning, and thy faithfulness every night,

"As a youth it was hard to understand Devotions. In school there are so many things in your studies. As I grew older and accepted the Lord and later when I became a Deacon, it became my responsibility to learn the scriptures because I wanted to share the word with the congregation. It is recorded in the word of the Lord, Timothy 2:15:-

" 'Study to shew thyself approved unto God, a workman that needeth not to be ashamed, rightly dividing the word of truth." meaning "Work hard so you can present yourself to God and receive his approval'."

"Back in those days the people in the Caicos islands made a living with farming and 'fishning' (fishing) and we produced vegetables.

"We would load the small sail boats and take our goods to Grand Turk. Salt Cay and Grand Turk had little land to farm and their principal industry was raking salt for export and so our fruit and vegetables sold well.

"I myself had a sloop, the famous **Windjammer**. All the people would load that boat up with charcoal. That's what everyone cooked with. They knew nothing about stoves like today.

"Anyway, we would make our trip from the Caicos loaded with charcoal, vegetables and fruits like potatoes, plantains and bananas, anything we could grow.

"We were four men crewing the boat. There was me, William Simmons and the late Christophe Forbes and also my brother Johnathan.

"We had a custom that we would sail during the day. We would leave Sandy Point for South Caicos and rest on the Bank for the night and then set sail again.

"People who are not familiar with the Bank need to be very careful because there are many dangerous rocks and shoals on the Banks, and many a boat has shipwrecked over time.

"From Sandy Point on my slow boat it would take two days to reach Grand Turk. You may think that the fruit would spoil and some did. We had a fruit we took on board called sapodilla.

"These we would pick from the farms when they were green. You would do this because you want the sapodillas to ripen on the sailboat. In this way when you arrived in Grand Turk they were not spoilt and you still had a market for them.

"It was very tricky... the longer we sailed the better it was. The people in Grand Turk were guaranteed that the sapodillas were ripe, in good condition and ready for the market.

"We all had different agents there... Missy Grant, Hattie Smith and a woman called Mary Skippings.

FISHING BOATS, NASSAU

"The other work men had around here was conching and sponging. All was very difficult but we had no choice. We all had our slow boats from Middle Caicos down to Blue Hills.

"From Sandy Point we would have to walk into Kew to go to the shops. There was Harold Robinson, he used to sell grocery and there was Isiah Wynns and another lady by the name of Tara Hall.

"Now if you went further along into Bottle Creek you had my grandmother and she had a little grocery store.

"I remember back in 1954, we used to dock in town called 'Town Dock' and right there near Timco was Governors Wharf.

"Back in those days you could see all of the harvested salt piled high on the shoreline with salt ships anchored off and waiting for delivery.

"Now, in Salt Cay, you could only get there in the Summer time and the seas could get rough especially getting into Dean's Dock.

"There was another man by the name of Duncanson. Now just to think that in order to get their supplies for the shops, they had to go in a boat to Grand Turk on a regular basis.

"This is how the men made a living. The women did the farming and the mens mainly did the 'fishning'.

"I mean by this that the men went out to sea to get the conchs and carry them to Haiti.

Artist Nina Shilling:
Town Dock, Grand Turk

"Middle Caicos, Bottle Creek, Blue Hills... we all did the same thing. In a way we were dependent on the Haitians.

"I also know a little about sponging. I used to work with a man by the name of Thomas Forbes. For short we used to call him 'Tommy' and I used to sail on the **City Queen** with him.

"Every Sunday evening we would leave from Bellefield Landing and go out on the Bank. Once we arrived, we would take up the sponge from the bottom. Then we would stack the sponge on the deck of the boat.

"By Friday evening we would come into shore. By then we had spent a whole week up on the Banks. Once on land we put all the sponge in a crawl and let the sponge soak.

"On Monday morning, giving it three days, we would wash that sponge out. We would continue cleaning until we get a near full cargo.

"When we got a cargo, then we would take that sponge from here to Nassau where the Greek agents would buy the sponge for little as nothing.

"When we got to Nassau we had to off-load that sponge and take it to a place that looked like a warehouse and stack that sponge up according to type.

"We had different types of sponge. We had grass sponge, wool sponge, yellow sponge and reef sponge. The agents would buy the sponge for near nothing, but I was only one of the crew and to be honest my interest was in getting my little money so I could spend it.

"Sailing on the sloop boats you had to have a four hour watch. That's why you have a crew, because sailing on the ocean can be dangerous and sometimes there's nowhere to anchor.

"We would sail all night and all day. Two men sleep, one man on the wheel and the other looking out... four hours on a watch and we would continue that until we got home. When we reached home the woman folk would be waiting to see what little things we traded for in Nassau, like colourful cloth, combs and rice.

LANDING SPONGES – NASSAU. BAHAMAS

"To tell you the truth, in the early morning and certainly on my boat we used to pray, and to pass time we would talk about life and how we were going to make it.

"I have been out in bad weather. One time I was out to Grand Turk and the wind went to North West. I was anchored off Governor's Wharf, there in town.

"I couldn't get out of the cut and when that cut is blocked up with the wave of the sea, there's no getting out.

"So, back in those days if the weather was rough we would go round on the Eastern side and try to make it to the Creek where the sea was calmer. It so happened that two sloops close to my own boat had their anchor drag and they came down on my sloop.

"All of us about to sink and I had to make a fast decision and decided to go to work and cut away my line and head for land.

"We came in on the Bay, there by Frankie Jones. I believe he used to work for Government. Anyway we managed to get the boat close to shore and when we did, me and a man by the name of William Simmons turned the boat so the wave could roll it landwards.

"I jumped out and took off to the nearby rum shop to fetch some men to help us.

"How lucky was I. When I returned to my boat there was a man standing there by the name of James Missick. He was the Captain or in charge of the Government boat.

"Jones, looking out across the Bay, had spotted us in trouble and sent for James Missick, so when I returned to the beach there was Missick with many men and a truck to help us pull the boat to shore.

"Together, they pulled my boat to safety and we all lived to sail another day!"

REENA LOUISE STUBBS PIERRE

From the Bight, took off to make a living in the Bahamas

"My name is Annerine Louise Stubbs Pierre and I was born on 21st October 1926 in the year of the terrible hurricanes which threw down all the houses and killed many people including my great grandmother Harriot Delancy.

"My mother was Muriel Delancy and she married James Pratt. He was more like my step dad, a very nice man who worked on the boats. My natural father was also a lovely man, a loving man and very kind and affectionate. He was a boatman.

"My people came from a long line of boating people and my granddaddy built the boat called the *PNT*.

"I will tell you that growing up in those days was rough, really rough. We lived in a little wooden house with a thatch roof.

"I lived in the house of my grandma and she had thirteen children. When I knew myself, I realized I was the eldest gran. It was tough. As the eldest I had the most work... there were plenty of chores.

"I had to wash, starch and iron for everyone and we had to tote water every day from the Bay. All the children would go to the well before school and carry the water back in a canister on our head.

"We woke early by five in the morning to get our chores done. First we got the water and then we fetched wood to put on the fire. The fire was built on three rocks... that's how we cooked back in the day, on three rocks, but let me tell you the food taste so good and every one helped each other.

"We weren't a pretty sight but we had to rush and get ready to make school by nine o'clock. We had to walk North side where Clement Howell School is now. It was a long walk.

"My teacher was Raymond Gardener. We sat on wooden desks and we would write with chalk on slate. I was not smart, I used to like to play too much, like hoopla and skip.

"I had a lot of friends from the neighbourhood, but they all died out now, but one of them was my cousin Rosina Hutchinson, a lovely, lively girl.

"At night, we all slept on the floor. It stayed that way until we grew up, moved out and made our own way.

"I moved out when my ma married and we lived right here on this rock, in this area which we all call the Bight.

"I grew up weeding grass, growing corn and doing farming. We worked on what we called plantations and we weeded the grass so we could turn it over and plant more things.

"We all went to Church every Sunday, the little one down by the school on the hill... the Jericho Baptist. We would wear cute little dresses and fix our hair. We would braid our hair.

"My granddaddy was the Deacon Peter Delancy and Joseph Stubbs was the head of the Church. We would sit on big benches. As you find, so you sit.

"When I was 20 years old, I went to the Bahamas to live with my aunt, Estella Delancy.

"It was shortly after the terrible hurricane of 45 when so many fisher boats were destroyed and there was no work.

Carrying rain water from the village well...

"People were hungry all about, and many islanders went to the Bahamas to make a better living and send money home for the family.

"Four of my aunts went, and we all lived close by on the same road in little clapboard houses. My aunt Estella had one, and from the first day I arrived she made me feel welcome.

"She was a very loving woman but within the space of a year she had lost her sight. She had no children, so I looked after her and she found me a little housekeeping job, cleaning houses and washing clothes.

"That's what we did to make a few shillings. We all used to do straw work making baskets, bags and hats and all kinds of little things.

"We would fancy up the hats with ribbons and braid and hang them up so that the tourists would buy one.

PLAITING BASKETS FROM PALMETTO STRAW, NASSAU, BAHAMAS.

"My mother Muriel was a difficult woman and often we did not see eye to eye but then again she had a hard life. She was a very strict woman and the problem was that she liked to beat a lot.

"She had eight children, four boys and four girls. There was my eldest brother Peter, Prince Albert, Joseph and Grovenor. There was me and my sisters, Dorothy, Anna May and Rosabelle.

"Now my great grandmother was a stooped-over white lady by the name of Harriot, the one I told you died in the hurricane. Who I remember most was my grandma Margaret Delancy who was light skinned with plenty of long hair and I was born in her hands.

"Growing up she would say work hard until you accumulate something. She was a strict woman but very nice. All the mens at the time were boatmen, fishing and conching and sailing to Haiti. Often too, they went to Grand Turk with charcoal, corn, hats, blades and baskets.

"When time to go Grand Turk on the boats, we would get potatoes out of the yard, grind the corn, make the grits and carry this to load on the big sail boats getting ready to set sail.

"When we got to Grand Turk and paid our little money we would go to the shops along the road and buy material, buy dress to wear for Sunday best.

"Sometimes we would go to Nassau. We would leave on a Saturday and get in there on Tuesday night and dock on the Wednesday morning.

"My grandaddy had a boat called the **PNT** and my step daddy James had one called the **Walton**. When we get in Nassau it was like a big city... here in the Bight was only a little place.

Nassau Street.

"Nassau seemed bright and busy. It was while I was in the Bahamas that I met my husband Charlie Pierre, but I came back home for a trip in 1973 to spend Christmas with my people.

"When I returned home for good, it was very hard for me to settle down. I don't like cooking so I would go in the field, eight o'clock morning time.

"You have to put wood under the pot to cook food and place the three rocks under it. They were for keeping the pots straight. Then you weed the grass all day.

"My grandma, I never remember her going to a doctor. They had women called midwives and when they had that baby, that house had to be closed up. House closed up with the mother in bed with baby.

"When the baby get nine days the mother would walk the baby round the house, cover up all the gaps in the windows and under the door. She couldn't leave the house.

"I remember one bush medicine my mother used was called 'stow-wood' called the 'devil coffee coneal'... you boil it and drink it.

"It's good for babies; if they have a cold you mix this in the milk. It's very bitter and we had to drink it or we were given a spanking.

"Going to school we had to take cod liver oil and then a little milk to follow. That's how rough life was.

"When I was in the Bahamas you got paper to make your own patterns. I would make some very pretty designs for the crochet work. We used to work with different coloured thread.

"I remember in my teens when we used to walk to 'Bottom Road' and cut the sisal. We would sliver it up, tie it down and carry it to 'Heaving Down Rock' where we would put it in the salt water and let the muck clean off it.

"You would beat it, wash it out and carry it home where you would dry it out, bundle it up and take it to the sailing boats leaving for Grand Turk.

"Once there, it was shipped out to foreign lands where it was made into rope. We had to tote the sugar cane, carry it on our heads and keep planting and cutting. The cane would grow high as this door. Those times were rough and when I say rough, I mean rough. I'm glad I got away when I did!

"As a final word, let me tell you my favorite Psalm... 'The Lord is my Shepherd', Psalm 23:-"

The Lord is My Shepherd
A Psalm of David.

The Lord is my shepherd; I shall not want.

He makes me to lie down in green pastures;
He leads me beside the still waters.

He restores my soul;
He leads me in the paths of righteousness
For His name's sake.

Yea, though I walk through the valley of the shadow of death,
I will fear no evil; For You are with me;
Your rod and Your staff, they comfort me.

You prepare a table before me in the presence of my enemies;
You anoint my head with oil; My cup runs over.

Surely goodness and mercy shall follow me
All the days of my life;
And I will dwell in the house of the Lord...Forever.

ALTON HIGGS FROM LORIMERS

The secret of long life

Juicing a carrot, apple and wheat grass will help our eyesight, keep the doctor away and help 'detox' the colon!

So imagine my delight when I heard that the most powerful energy drink is actually found in the old settlement of Lorimers in Middle Caicos and is concocted by Alton Robertson Higgs, a 'local bush doctor' born on October 17, 1920.

What a character! He greeted me with a strong handshake, hearty laugh and a personality that matched the many bright, hand-woven mats that covered almost every spare space on his floors and walls.

Every colourful mat was made from drift rope that he collected from walks along the beach and shores of his home.

"I spend all my years here in Lorimers. We have always been a fishing and farming community. We were never a lazy people. We would farm and fish so's we could hook a wife," he laughed.

"My father was Benjamin Higgs from North Caicos and my mother's name was Isadora Missick from right here in Middle.

"I loved to walk and sometimes too, we would dive for craw-fish over in the creek. They was plentiful. We had no mask or goggles back then... when we dived down we had to meet them crawfish with our eyes!

Alton continued on nonplussed. "In those times my father was a foreman on a Dutch ship and my mother was home doing all the farming. Sometimes she would be working all week in the sisal plantations in Jacksonville on East Caicos.

"As a boy I also worked in the sisal fields. We would have to cut it, strip it down and carry it to the creek and put the sisal in the water to soak.

"It took about two weeks to wash the fibre out good. If you were in a hurry for it then it would take about eight days. After you wash the sisal then you would put it out to dry.

"Back then we had two men that would receive the sisal, Simon Hall and his brother Peter who was a policeman at that time. Sometimes there was a woman over in South Caicos called Amy Stubbs who would collect the sisal. She had the house on the hill. They were the agents.

"Then the government took over and I went to sea, fishing and conching for a livin' all about, and often went to Milton Cay. I had my own sailboat back then which was built by Mr Albert Outten. Yeah man.

"I spent the Hurricane of 1945 with my gang of friends from Lorimers under our dinghy over on Milton Cay. There was David Hall, William Penn and many others but there was nothing we could do but lay cool, wait for the weather to subside, and pray to God.

"When we finally arrived home to Middle Caicos we saw that plenty of homes were 'mash up.'

"Anyway," said Alton changing the subject rapidly and before I could get a handle on the '45 hurricane. "All young people must have vision and get back to their roots. Our forefathers laid the foundation of these islands and young people must embark on hard work because they can do anything they want these days."

"You mean the world is their oyster?" said I. We both had to think for a long moment and decided to switch subjects again while we pondered this question.

"It was my mother that would teach me about plants. There was no doctors or nurses back then, we came up on the bush medicine. Yeah man, on the turning of the moon, my mother would boil the bush tea in special bottles and give it to us for the worms.

"We had many bush medicines. We had the catnip and the snake-stick, good for indigestion and the stomach, and for fever too.

"Now the 'bay-tansy' out on Long Bay was used for pregnant women and was used to help with the delivery. It was good for the hair and good for the bowels and indigestion.

85

"We even had a cure for mosquitoes," he laughed. "We would burn cow dung in our little pots and the smoke would keep the mosquitoes away."

"So what's the most powerful bush medicine there is?" I asked.

"Well for the power part I have it right here." And Alton pointed to a tall glass bottle in the corner of his room.

"The secret to good health," he said, "is hard work and what's here in this bottle," as he poured me a glass of Marby with great attention and pride.

"Round here we call it M.B. for short. It's a power drink straight from the bush. Anyone can drink it, man, woman, girl and even strangers!

"It cleans you out and goes right in the blood. Yeah man, it gives you plenty energy," he said with his deep hearty laugh and a twinkle in his eye.

"Come on Alton," I insisted, "you can tell me what secret ingredients are in this Marby concoction, the secret of long life and the way to become a millionaire!"

Mr. Alton Higgs alias the bushman just looked me straight in the eye and said: "Wonderful power and God's blessing... I need not tell you anymore."

THE BROWN PELICAN

National bird of the Turks and Caicos Islands

"Oh, a wondrous bird is the pelican,
His bill can hold more than his belican,
He can take in his beak,
Food enough for a week,
But I'm damned if I see how the helican".

The Caribbean Brown Pelican, or *Pelecanus occidentalis,* is an aquatic bird and lives in warm tropical climates.

It is the smallest of eight species of pelican, although it is large for a shoreline bird. These birds love to inhabit the coastlines and rarely fly more than twenty miles out to sea.

Many Brown Pelicans can be seen on most of the islands of the Turks and Caicos, which are an ideal fishing ground for these remarkable birds. They are often spotted sitting on posts near harbours and docks. Everyone enjoys watching the Brown Pelican, which is awkward on land and elegant in flight.

They certainly have cartoon type features because of their large flattened bills and its distensible pouch used for engulfing fish.

The 'gular' pouch as it is called is found on the lower side of the bill and is essential for draining water when it scoops fish out of the sea.

In fact these pelicans dive from on high and swoop down in a sudden plunge that stuns the unsuspecting prey with amazing speed, force and accuracy.

Extensive use of pesticides nearly depleted the pelican population but today they are growing in numbers, nesting in colonies on mainly inaccessible coastal islands.

The pelicans migrate along the shores of the Caribbean preferring the sunny climates of spring and summer during the breeding season.

Both the male and female pelicans participate in incubation, which adds warmth and protection from predators seeking out nests with unattended eggs.

Conch pearls, or 'pink pearls' as they are called, are one of the rarest and most valuable types of pearl in the world.

Out of some 10,000 shells or more, fishermen may find one solitary pearl produced by the Queen Conch mollusk.

Many visitors to these islands are fascinated by the beautiful pink shell of the Queen Conch (*Strombus gigas*) which walked the sea grass beds in shallow tropical waters long before the Taino Indians inhabited the Turks and Caicos, and fished for conch as part of their staple diet.

Over-harvesting of conch in the region has been a problem for many years. As a result today, the export of conch is illegal without a permit.

The queen conch is protected under the international CITES treaty (Convention on International Trade in Endangered Species), which includes species not necessarily threatened with extinction but in need of monitoring and control.

Queen conchs (pronounced 'konks') are soft-bodied animals: in fact large edible sea snails belonging to the same group (Mollusca) as clams, oysters, octopuses and squid and are native to the Florida Keys, Bahamas, Turks and Caicos and Bermuda. They are herbivores eating algae, tiny plankton and marine plants.

The queen conchs reach maturity after five years, at which point the male and female can mate.

THE LUSTROUS PINK PEARL

of the Queen Conch

She lays thousands of tiny eggs in the sand and a few days later, the larvae emerge and drift in the currents.

After twenty eight days the larvae finally settle on the seabed and for the next year live under the sand, coming out at night to feed.

However, many conch are lost to natural predators like nurse sharks, turtles, eagle-rays, lobsters and crabs. For local fisherman, diving for conch is a way of life embedded in the culture, and in the delicious local cuisine where conch rules supreme.

HOLTON DICKENSON

Growing up on the salt raking island of Salt Cay in the mid 1900s

"My ma, Ethel Louise Been was a very kind and friendly person married to my father Manfred Milton Dickenson and her mother was Katherine married to Fred Been. Ma was from the South District and was a good cook.

"In those days they would kill a cow and a pig almost every Saturday. Then you would go round to Ms Robinson and get a lb of cow liver. Sometimes you would have a plate of peas, homini and conch.

"At that time we used to tote water on our heads. We had these canisters and walked often to the main government tank to fetch the rain water. People didn't have much of their own tanks then. When the government tanks got dry we were put on rations and had to walk way South to the wells to tote water home. Sometimes you had to wash your clothes down at the wells.

"I grew up in Salt Cay and when I was seven attended the Government School. My teacher was Ronald Jones. We used to call him 'Boney.' He was a very good teacher and a good dresser, always in khaki pants. He came from South Caicos to help Christy Jennings who worked in the Government Office.

"I remember my class mates Ruphine Glinton, Audrey Taylor, Lloyd Williams, George Been, Joseph Smith, Willy Jennings and a girl by the name of Willa Seymour from South.

"After Ronald, came Ms Mary Robinson. She would never let us skylark, a strict and clever teacher who taught us all the subjects.

"Most of us never went to high school because you had to pay and we couldn't afford it. Only Alfred Been and Bart Williams went to high school because they were sponsored.

"My father used to work almost every day in the salinas raking salt for the grumpy and mean Howard Harriott, a salt merchant who owned the White House, now a historic landmark on Salt Cay.

"He would go out at six in the morning after a little tea and at nine o clock he would come home for breakfast and back to work by ten. There was a break at one o'clock for lunch and then the men worked straight through til sundown.

"It was very hard work because the pickle would be hot. Each day my pa would put on slippers made from old rubber tires to help ward against the hot and sharp salt in the ponds. The rubber slippers would be wrapped with string to hold the so-called shoes in place and were called 'whompers.'

"You would always wear a straw hat which the men got from the Caicos islands. Inside the straw hat you would wear a broad grape leaf from the Bay to protect the eyes from the harsh dazzling sun. There was no shades back then and sun and salt are too strong for the eyes.

'Salt Raker'
Salt Cay

"They would wear Bagan, three quarter length shorts which were made from cotton. The men would collect their tools, rakes, shovels and pickaxes from the White House yard. Their boss Mr Franklyn Harriot was not a kind man and worked them hard.

"He never went to Church but he might stop you on a Sunday and say, 'Paint my boat.' He had seven or eight boats like the **Achilles**, **New Era**, **Palastinia** and the **Enterprise.**

Salt Merchant Home
Brown House

Harriott family outside the
Brown House

"Franklyn's father Skipper Harriot lived down at the Brown House. He was a very mean old man and only had one eye. The other was made of marble that he would take out at night and keep by his bedside.

"So one day my father sent me down there to sell some eggs to Winnie his wife, who was very kind... she would buy the eggs and sometimes give you a little flour or sugar.

"As I reached the Brown House this particular morning, Skipper was coming down the steps noisily with his walking stick, groop... groop... groop wearing his usual attire, top hat, full suit and pocket watch in his vest.

"His wife saw me and motioned for me to hide out the way. So I hide under the stairs on his bad eye.

"When he crossed to go to his payroll office, I clambered the stairs to the kindly Ms Winnie who bought my eggs. It was always an ordeal at the Brown House.

"In fact, let me give you another story about old Skipper.

"One day he had to go to Grand Turk to collect some payroll money and to attend one of the regular meetings concerning the salt industry.

"Once he finished his tasks, collected the men's pay and gathered the crew, they left Grand Turk for Salt Cay in what they called a Dublin boat with six oars. There were Tombolly, Manuel Simmons, James and a couple of others.

"It was a fair, moderate day but they came in too high on the reef, right there by Cotton Cay and a sudden swell came in and bust the boat. Old Skipper could not swim so Manuel stayed with him.

"Manuel and Skipper were last seen hanging onto the side of the boat while Tombolly and Jama decided to swim for shore. In fact, Tombolly was a strong swimmer and had to help Jama reach shore as he was beginning to fail. They staggered onto North Beach and walked all the way into town to fetch help but by then night was falling!

"In those days many men drowned at sea as the gales and high seas came quickly and as yet the men had no navigational equipment to guide them around the reefs. My father also drowned while out fishing one Saturday.

"It was the habit that me and my father used to go fishing every Saturday. On Friday afternoons I would go down South on the beach and get some periwinkles and whelks to bait up with, so that in the morning round about eight or nine o'clock we would go fishing.

"We had a small boat that my father would borrow from Jody Kennedy. Well this Friday my father had been working in the salt ponds and he told me he was going fishing with Kaleb instead, and that I could go with little Jimmy Garland.

"My pa and Kaleb set off in a sail boat for Sand Cay which is a ways away but they always planned to return by 1pm. Meanwhile, me and Jimmy took the small sculling dinghy round by the Barren Ground.

"I remember the day, September the 13th when a sudden gale wind sprung up and our boat was dragged onto the bank. It was raining hard but we managed to skull the boat up on Saunders where we threw the anchor down and waited til the wind blew off.

"It must have been during that time that my father and Kaleb were coming down from Sand Cay when the gale wind capsized their boat.

"In those days they had rocks inside the boat for ballast to keep the sail steady.

"So when the gale hit that boat it turned the boat right over and they would have held onto the sides for a good little while. Trouble was that on South Point there is a strong current and it sweeps you out.

"We never saw the men again. That afternoon the boats went out to look for them, but they were nowhere in sight.

"I was just 19 years old and still in apprenticeship with Josey Jones, that was Clifford Jones' father. I used to stay with him and Mary Robinson. I would go to the wells for water, look after the fowls and take care of the animals.

"Now two days after my pa died I moved back to the house to take care of ma and my sisters. By that Monday I had to replace my father and go in the ponds to rake salt. My job was to break up salt in the big pond. There were plenty of ponds along the folly that belonged to the Harriotts and the Morgans.

"Josey Jones had a couple of ponds he worked. Roddy Robinson had a pond he worked for the Mullins over-back somewhere. The Talbots had a little pond. Then you had Pitchers Hole... that was for the Smiths, Henry Smith, Alfred Smith, one fella from Puerto Plata called Isaac Smith and their sister Amy married to Kaleb Simmons. The Smiths would send their salt to Jamaica.

Salt pans on Salt Cay

"Along Victoria St were two salt sheds to store salt from the bad weather. One was for the poor people, right there where Pat's shop is now. It was a huge salt shed in three sections and salt deposits could be seen all along the shoreline.

"Salt was usually shoveled into half-bushel burlap bags and loaded into the small sail boats, what we call 'lighters.' There wasn't a natural harbour on Salt Cay for large vessels so the lighters had to sail out to the ships anchored on the edge of the deep.

"All day long the lighters went back and forth with over 400 salt bags on every trip. It was hard work and come sundown you had to remove the masts, the sails and the rigging which were stored in the loft above the boat house. Below, the boats were kept for safety.

"In my time, there was another method of loading salt. The salt was loaded into a rail cart from the White House basement and trammed to the wharf where it was loaded into a chute that flowed directly into the holds of what we also called the box boat.

"Once loaded, the lighter sailed out to the waiting ships. In my father's day the ships were two and half mast schooners from Nova Scotia and huge tugs from Newfoundland where they salted cod fish.

Loading salt into the box lighter at Harriott's Wharf, Salt Cay

Sam Smith and his mule George

"I worked in the ponds for quite a while until I got work as a carpenter's helper with Joseph Kennedy.

"The workshop was next to the White House on Victoria Street and close by thirteen mules were stabled and looked after by Sam Smith. There was plenty of work fixing the cart wheels.

Taking the burlap sacks of salt out
to the waiting ships,
Salt Cay

Cargo Ship, the *Berkshire*

MANY MEN WENT TO SEA TO MAKE A LIVING

New York-based National Bulk Carriers was owned by an American entrepreneur by the name of Daniel Keith Ludwig (1897-1992).

It was Ludwig who pioneered the construction of super tankers including many of the tankers that Turks island men sailed on like the **Ore Venus**, **Ore Jupiter**, **Universe Commander**, **Ulysses** and near fifty-five other ships.

Beside ship construction he founded Exportadora de Sal at Guerrero De Negro lagoon in Mexico which developed the largest salt company in the world.

Salt flats in Guerrero Negro, Mexico

"With the salt trade failing", said Holton Dickinson, "many Turks islanders chose to go to sea and travel around the world, sending money home to their families.

"It was the mid 1900s and with the global growth of trade and production, the ships became bigger and more cost effective. New technology in containerization and bulkification of natural products meant an increasing demand for labourers and seamen.

"At the time," continued Holton, "I lived by Mary Robinson, and her nephew Nathanial Robinson who was the agent for National Bulk Carriers. They had an agent in the Caymans and an agent here and Nathaniel aka Netty would hire the men from Salt Cay and Grand Turk.

"So Ms Robinson talked to Netty and secured me, Herbert Simmons, Randal Moore and many other men a job to go sailing on the huge tankers carrying grain, crude oil, salt and iron ore.

"The first ship I went on was the **Berkshire** in the early 60s. I was a mess man for the officers. We would transport the salt from Mexico to Tacoma, a port city along Washington's Puget Sound.

"After ten months at sea and a short spell at home I went Eastwards on the **Ore Venus** built in the 1960s. Her length was 571 feet and as the name suggests was a class ore carrier transporting iron ore, from and to the Americas.

"Aboard the **Ore Venus** we would sail to Venezuela where the iron ore was shipped from Puerto Ordaz on the Orinoco River to the Port of Philadelphia on the Delaware River.

"There was always plenty of activity in the docks loading and off-loading of other commodities like steel and coal.

"We would sometimes go to Baltimore, Mobile Alabama and Italian ports like Piombino and Genoa in Italy.

"So many ships. I remember the super tankers. We would leave from Trinidad to the Persian Gulf carrying crude oil, and on the way we would round Cape Horn at the southern tip of South America.

"It was a long and dangerous shipping route which avoided the Panama Canal. The sea gets so rough and the winds so strong.

"Other voyages took us down the Suez Canal which runs through Egypt and connects the Mediterranean Sea to the Red Sea. It cut down on sailing time and made the Suez the shortest maritime route to Asia from Europe.

"This time I was working on the **Bulk Trader** carrying oil. We would arrive at Port Said on the Northern end of the Suez and wait for experienced Egyptian sailors who were designated to help us navigate through the narrow channel of the Canal.

"One of the reasons was the size of the oil tanker and another was the terrible sand storms which blew up regularly with almost blind visibility. The Egyptians kept the ship on course.

"The last ship I sailed on was the **Universe Commander.** I believe there was Shirlin Garland, Baron Skippings, Terrance Missick, Spike Saunders, Richard Williams and many other locals on-board.

"I was at sea for over fifteen years until I returned to my family on Salt Cay."

Image Index and References

3. Damedias (Graphic).Coral Reef and Tropical Fish [2020] . http://Stock.adobe.com

5. Shilling, N. 2020. (Watercolour). Crabbing in Middle Caicos [Commissioned]://flamingoislandbooks.com

10. Florida Images, 2015 (Photo). Great Blue Crab. [2019] http://Alamy.com

11. Block, F. 2014. (Photo). Repairing the Nets. [2019]. http://Stock.adobe.com

16. Read, E J, 1907 (Watercolour).Street Scene Nassau [2021] Born 1860, death unknown

17. Read, E J, 1907 (Watercolour). A Sponge Clipper [2021] Born 1860, death unknown

20. Visit http://www.westindianboas.org/west-indian-boas/genus-chilabothrus/chrysogaster

23. The Keasbury-Gordon photograph Archive, c1930 (photo).Cutting Sisal.[2019] http:Alamy.com

25. Pulsar Imagen. 2015 (photo). Donkey loaded with Sisal. [2019].http://Alamy.com

30. Ramsey, Allan (Photo). King George III in Coronation Gown [2020] https://commons.wikimedia.org

31. Nider Picture Library,(engraving). Call to Arms, American Revolution [2022] http://Alamy.com

31. Nider Picture Library,(engraving). Call to Arms, American Revolution [2022] http://Alamy.com

35. Walker, W A. 1800s. (Painting). Boy holding a Cotton Bale [2020] https://oridesmjr-blogspot-com

40. Shilling, N 2021. (Watercolour). Hunting for Sponge in the Caicos Islands [Commissioned]

41. Granger, NYC/Granger Historical Archive.(photo). Sponge Fleet [2019] http://Alamy.com

41. Granger, NYC/Granger Historical Archive.(photo). Sponge Fleet [2019] http://Alamy.com

44. Beaubelle/Alamy. (Vector). 2015. Cuban Crows on a Branch [2022] http://Alamy.com

44. Beaubelle/Alamy. (Vector). 2015. Cuban Crows on a Branch [2022] http://Alamy.com

47. Shilling, N, 2022 (Water colour). six Man boat, Spearing a Whale (Commissioned 2022)

50. Jamaican steamship http://Alamy.com

52. Winterhalter, 1842. F X. (Painting) The Young Queen Victoria [2022] https://commons.wikimedia.org

56. De Freitas, M. 2015. (Photo). Methodist Church, Grand Turk. [2020} http://Alamy.com

57. Griese,E. The Frith Collection (Photo) Francis Streeter, First Wife of BC Frith.

58. Griese,E. The Frith Collection (Photo). Virginia Sawyer Frith and BC Frith

60. Herwin, C. 2012, Candy Herwin Collection (Photo). Ladies from the South

61. Shilling, N 2021 (Watercolour). Catching Turtles on the Bay. [Commissioned 2021]

64. Feiferman, P, 2016. (Photo). Donkey by Deans Dock, Salt Cay: https://www.tcmuseum.org

65. Rosalie Harriott Collection/TCI Museum. 1940 (photo). Water Carrier on Salt Cay://www.tcmuseum.org

67. Rosalie Harriott Collection/TCI Museum. 1940 (photo). Water Carrier on Salt Cay://www.tcmuseum.org

67. Oscar Talbot Collection/TCI Museum. 1940s (photo). Norman Talbot holding Fish://www.tcmuseum.org

69. Shilling, N. 2022 (Pen Drawing). Bone Fish in the Caicos. [Commissioned 2022]

71. Posner, L 2022 (Crayon Drawing). Drying Da Conch. [Commissioned 2022]

75. Shilling, N. 2021 (Watercolour). Unloading Salt, Town Dock, Grand Turk. [Commissioned 2021]

76. 1906. (Postcard) Sponge Yard along the Docks, Nassau, [Personal Collection]

76. 1906. (Postcard) Sponge Fishing Fleet. Nassau, [Personal Collection]

78. Herwin, C, 2022. (Pen). Young girl carrying water cannister: http://www.flamingoislandbooks.com

86. Anderson, J. 2004 (Photo). Brown Pelican. [2022] http://Alamy.com

89. Davis, E, 2017. (Water Colour). The Sloop *Enterprise* carrying salt

90. Shilling, N/ 2021. (Water Colour).The Brown House. [Commissioned 2021]

92. Rosalie Harriott Collection/ TCI Museum. c1930 (Photo). Sam on donkey .//www.tcmuseum.org

94. Shilling, N/ 2022. (Cargo Ship, the Berkshire. [Commissioned 2022]

95. Gunter Grafenhain/Mau ritius images (photo). Tanker between Sand Dunes [2022] http://Alamy.com

98. Posner, L. 2022 (Crayon Drawing). Unloading Salt Grand Turk [Commissioned 2022]

Edwin Lightbourne, last boat builder
on Salt Cay

AUTHOR: Candy Herwin

"One passion of mine is recording the history and culture of these islands through the narratives of the older folk before their history is lost forever.

Story telling is the ancient art of sharing knowledge with an engaged audience. Slowly however, this form of communicating is disappearing from the remote islands as the modern day challenges of survival fragment family and community life.

Perhaps, it is the duty of everyone to keep these stories circulating and to consciously be involved in the wellbeing of the community in which you live..."

www.flamingoislandbooks.com

Made in the USA
Columbia, SC
25 January 2023

10425170R10058